The Power
of a New
Identity

The Power of a New Identity

Overcoming a Broken Self-Image

Dan Sneed

Sovereign World

Published by Sovereign World Ltd
PO Box 784
Ellel
Lancaster LA1 9DA
United Kingdom

www.sovereignworld.com

ISBN 978-1-85240-636-3

Typeset by CRB Associates, Potterhanworth, Lincolnshire

Contents

	Foreword	7
	Acknowledgments	9
	Introduction	11
Chapter 1	A Tale of Men and Grasshoppers	17
Chapter 2	It Was Meant to Be So Different	25
Chapter 3	Who Do You Think You Are?	39
Chapter 4	My Dog, Spot, and the Strongholds of His Life	59
Chapter 5	Your Parents and You	78
Chapter 6	Life Experiences	90
Chapter 7	The Power of Forgiveness	102
Chapter 8	Leaving Your Past Behind	119
Chapter 9	The Mask Maker's Game	131
Chapter 10	Working It Out: Practical Steps to Changing Your Self-Image	159
Chapter 11	Free at Last!	180
Appendix	Who Am I in Christ?	185
	About the Author	191

Foreword

I want you to sit down for a visit with one of the most loving, patient encouragers I've ever known—Dan Sneed.

That ministry "office," if you will—Encourager—is, without a doubt, one of the most needed today. And it's a role that is too seldom described or honored for what it really is: It's Holy Spirit-like.

That's not a term I can remember hearing before, but when I was asked to write these few words to introduce Dan and his ministry to others, that's what came to mind.

We're all accustomed to hearing godly, thoughtful, caring, serving people described as "Christ-like" (and Dan is that, too), but I am focusing on the other terminology for two reasons.

First, the term *Holy Spirit-like* fits for a very academic reason. The verb root behind the Holy Spirit's title as "Comforter" essentially involves the practice of "encouraging." In other words, when Jesus decided to give His most detailed description of the One whom He would send to His Church after His ascension, He spoke of the Comforter–Encourager. Thus, to be a person committed to encouraging others is, in my words, to be "Holy Spirit-like."

Second, I wanted to use this description for a very practical reason. We all have occasion to meet people who speak about "being filled with the Holy Spirit" and are either too mystical, too other-worldly, too-busy-being-"spiritual"-to-do-anyone-any-good or—summarily put—too impractical. But in reality, a truly Spirit-filled person will be among the most realistic, down-to-earth, pragmatic and helpful people you'll ever meet. Spirituality isn't weird: It works!

And it's on the grounds of these two observations about Dan Sneed that I describe him as I have. I've known him for over thirty years. I've been his pastor, his co-worker, his fellow shepherd in Los Angeles and an observer of his missionary work, and I am as informed about his role as a husband and father as anyone. And in all of these demanding pursuits—in family, with friends or in ministry—Dan is a faithful, trustworthy, loving encourager.

So there you are. And here he is with encouragement for you.

After you've found out how right my description is, write him and tell him. He's the same as all the rest of us. He could use the encouragement, too.

Jack Hayford
President/Pastor
The King's Seminary
The Church on the Way

Acknowledgments

It Takes a Team

Like so many things, a book is never the project of just one person. It takes a team of committed people who invest a significant part of their lives and their gifting to make the project successful. I am so thankful for just such a team—thankful not only for those who have worked with me on this book, but also for a team of committed relationships that have helped me discover how to "Expose the Lie." I am convinced that discovering our identities in Jesus requires not only an element of divine revelation, but also some divine relationships as well. I have been blessed with both.

I will always be grateful for my wonderful parents, George and Celia Sneed, who invested so much of their lives in me. Every child should be so blessed. I am also grateful for my grandparents, especially my grandmother, Lucy Mae Sneed. Her relationship with Jesus and her love for me were the spiritual anchor of my life. She believed in me—and in God's power to make something of my life.

I am also grateful for the gift of Beverly Carlson, who became my wife more than thirty years ago. No one could love me like she does. Her committed, affirming love has helped define the power of a new identity, not only for me, but also for our children, Robert (who still likes to be called Bobby), Russell, Becky and Debbie. I like to think that as a father, I have taught them so much, but the reality is that I have learned far more through them than I ever imagined possible. They have taught me so much about the Father-heart of God, as well as the importance of understanding who we are in Him. Doug and Ken, the boys that God brought into our lives early in our marriage, were also a gift of God to me. Through all of the hard times and difficult moments, God taught us about unconditional love and commitment, as well as His ability to redeem.

One of the greatest gifts to me came through a relationship that developed while I was in Bible college. At a time when I was struggling out of a very deep inferiority complex, Pastor Doug Bjerke became an incredible tool of encouragement, affirmation and, at times, tough love. I will always be thankful for the gift he has been in building and shaping who I am today.

When I stop to realize all the people that God has used to impact my life, I am overwhelmed with gratitude. I wish time and space would allow me to mention all of them by name. But it's a list that never seems to end, and each person on it is extremely important to me—friendships that shaped my life and people who believed in me. I love them all.

I also want to thank my friend Greg Beastrom, who has not only been a great source of encouragement to me personally, but who has also given endless hours working on this manuscript. Without him, this book would not have been possible. He made sense out of my scribbling, and for that, I am grateful.

To the guys at Chosen Books and Sovereign World who pursued me to write this book and patiently waited for the project to be completed, thank you!

You see? It does take a team—a team to help you discover who God has made you to be and to help you walk through life with a sense of belonging and success. Moreover, it takes a team to write a book—and I am very grateful for mine.

Introduction

My plane had just landed at Dulles International Airport in Washington, D.C., for a brief stopover before continuing on to Amsterdam. It was to be one of those quick, just-enough-time-to-change-planes kinds of stopovers. The clock was running, and I was anxious to find a gift shop in order to buy my wife a card and get it into the mail before boarding the next flight. I really wanted to surprise her, and I knew that getting a card from me would certainly do that, if not induce a major coronary!

My wife is so much better at this sort of thing than I am. As a matter of fact, that very morning, I had settled into my seat on the flight to Washington and opened my briefcase, and there it was—a card from my beautiful wife, encouraging me and letting me know how much she loves me. She is always so wonderful, and I wanted so much to express to her how much she means to me.

I made it to the gift shop and found the card I was looking for. It said everything I wanted to say. In fact, it was perfect!

Then, as I stood in line waiting to pay for my wife's card, a curious thing happened. I was glancing around rather nonchalantly, when my eyes fell upon another card with these bold words at the top: *"I believe in you!"*

What a statement! What an affirmation! Immediately I began to think of several people I knew were all experiencing difficult circumstances and who desperately needed to hear that message.

I thought of one of my sons who, at the time, was struggling through his teenage years and needed to know that his dad believed in him.

I thought of a young pastor in another part of the world whose wife had just left him for another man, leaving him to raise their three kids by himself. Their youngest was only a few months old! This pastor needed to know that someone was standing with him through this heartbreaking situation.

I thought of another young man, a teenager in our church, who had just received Jesus and had been baptized only a few weeks before. He was living in a group home, alienated from his family and struggling with the brokenness of his life. He needed to know that he was at the forefront of my thoughts and prayers.

Each of these young men desperately needed the message of that card: *"I believe in you!"*

I do not recall how many "I believe in you!" cards there were at that counter, perhaps seven or eight, but I bought all of them that day. I have often wondered what the cashier was thinking when I went to check them all out: one card for my wife and a stack of "I believe in you!" cards for everyone else. I half-expected her to ask me, "Just how many people do you believe in?!" I did find a use for each of those cards immediately—all but one. I decided to keep one in my briefcase as a reminder to myself that we all need people who believe in us.

At the risk of being misunderstood by some, please allow me to ask you an important question: **Do you know that God believes in you?** He does! In fact, He believes in you so much, He paid the ultimate price—His life—so that you can have the opportunity of intimate fellowship with your Creator (see John 3:16; Romans 5:8).

I realize that saying, "God believes in you," can be misconstrued, so it is important for me to clarify what I mean. I am not implying that God puts His faith and trust in you. He is far too wise for that. What I am saying, however, is that God has never lost sight of who He created you to be, nor has He abandoned His original intent, that man created in His likeness would partner with Him in ruling over the earth.

So great is God's love for mankind and so glorious is man's intended destiny in comparison to the hopelessness of the human condition, that all of the wisdom and resources of heaven were made available for man's redemption. Indeed, the Father is absolutely determined that hell's diabolical plot to destroy our destiny will not succeed, to the point that He has provided for our forgiveness and reconciliation through His Son, Jesus Christ. It is with that understanding that I say, "God believes in you!"

Certainly that is knowledge enough to give you hope, but I have only scratched the surface!

When you receive Christ, not only does He give you a new identity (the foundation of every good thing that will follow), but He sends His Holy Spirit to reside within you in order to make possible the fulfillment of your destiny. In no uncertain terms, He is committed to you!

"For I am confident of this very thing, that He who began a good work in you will perfect it until the day of Christ Jesus" (Philippians 1:6). If nothing else, I want this book to speak hope to you, loud and clear! Regardless of what you have been through, how confused you may be, how broken your life is or how deep your desperation, never forget that there is more grace in God's heart than there is sin or brokenness in yours. In truth, His light is far more powerful than your darkness could ever be.

Our enemy, Satan, likes nothing more than to distort and confuse our image of who we are in Christ. He lies to us, trying to convince us that we are worthless, we are hopeless and we will never manage to enter into the fullness of all that God has for us in Christ. This book seeks to expose the lies of the enemy by presenting clearly the truth about your identity in Christ and the way that God feels about you.

In this book, I want to challenge you in two ways. First, I challenge you to believe the truth of what God says about you—that you are a new creation with a new identity. Accepting this truth is the basis of a profound struggle in the lives of most believers. God says that we are new creatures, but our minds often assail us with all the negative images of our past, as well as all the lies the kingdom of darkness has perpetuated about us throughout our lives. Overcoming these lies and images is a process that takes time, discipline and diligence. It is a challenge, but one worth taking.

The second challenge, I believe, is key to the effectiveness of the Church in the 21st century. We live in a society in which feeling good is everything. "I've got to feel good about me" is the motive behind much of the self-help movement.

There is no question about it. You should feel good about who God has made you to be, but the purpose of a right self-image is far greater than that. I want to challenge you to become everything God has made you to be, not just as an investment in yourself, but as an investment in the lives of others! Be a servant! In other words, be a person who spends his or her life making others successful, releasing his or her God-given potential and touching a broken, needy world with the healing love of Jesus. That is what *Exposing the Lie* is all about.

One more thing before you begin reading. Keep in mind that you are assured success at being who God made you to be! Remember: "For I am confident of this very thing, that He who began a good work in you will perfect it until the day of Christ Jesus" (Philippians 1:6). As you walk through the process of healing and restoration, remember that God has the ability to accomplish in you all that He has promised—and He is committed to doing exactly that.

I have heard it said that success as a believer depends more on God's ability as a teacher than it does on our abilities as students. If that is true—and I am convinced that it is—then we have cause for great hope!

"Now to Him who is able to do exceedingly abundantly above all that we ask or think, according to the power that works in us, to Him be glory in the church by Christ Jesus to all generations, forever and ever. Amen" (Ephesians 3:20–21).

Chapter 1

A Tale of Men and Grasshoppers

Have you ever imagined what God's voice must sound like? I have! In fact I've heard a voice I'm sure must sound like God's. Even though I can't remember exactly what he said, the first time I heard Dr. Lloyd Ogilvie speak, his voice captured my attention. I remember saying to myself, "That's the voice of God! That's what God must sound like!"

At that time, he was the pastor of the Hollywood Presbyterian church. Later, he went on to be chaplain of the United States Senate. His voice is deep and rich and very classy. If you have ever heard it you would never forget it. He grew up in Scotland, and you know how classy a Scottish gentleman's voice can sound. However, most of his adult life has been in the United States, so his voice has become very clear to an American audience. He is the man, I think, that sounds like God. In fact, when I get to heaven, if God doesn't sound like Lloyd Ogilvie, I may not recognize His voice.

Not only did his voice captivate me the first time I heard it, but the story he told left a deep impression that I'll never forget. Shortly after he became the pastor of Hollywood Press, an elderly member of his congregation took him by the hand, looked into his eyes and spoke these words: "I pray that your life will be as wonderful as it was in the mind of God when He created you."

With those words locked in his mind, he went to his study, got down on his knees, and asked, "What did You have in mind when You created me?"

Clearly just one word came flooding in: "Jesus. I created you to be like My Son Jesus."

That story and those words, "I pray that your life will be as wonderful as it was in the mind of God when He created you" left an incredibly strong impression on me. I wrote them down in my Bible and I have prayed them over people all over the world. I believe God has a dream for each one of our lives, and His dream is good! I also believe He has given each one of us everything we need to become all He has created us to be. Life is not always wonderful—we all know that. Things happen that can have a devastating impact on our lives. The circumstances around us, things we have little control over, choices that others make, especially significant people in our lives and, yes, the choices we make, all affect the fulfillment of His dream and what we experience in everyday life.

Recently, I rode through the streets of Port Au Prince, Haiti, witnessing first hand, the devastation of the largest natural disaster to ever hit the Western Hemisphere. What caught my attention was not the rubble of thousands of collapsed buildings or the stench of garbage that permeated the air. Nor was it the massive tent cities where tens of thousands live in the aftermath of the earthquake. It was the faces of those whose life experience was anything but what God intended for His creation. People marked by the wounds of life—wounds that shaped their very existence.

Years ago, I listened as a young boy poured out his deep anger and hurt toward his father who deserted him as an infant. He began the conversation with a painful question: "Why does my father hate me . . . what did I do wrong?"

You see, life isn't always wonderful. Sometimes the wounds of our lives speak so loudly, they drown out the promise.

They lock up our potential. They transform our dream into hopelessness. In this young boy's case, I knew his father and knew that his father in no way hated him. His father is a very broken man. However, in a young boy's mind, the fact his father left when he was an infant and has not contacted him creates a deep wound. The wound sends this message: "My father hates me and it's my fault." And that lie is believed.

With every wound in our life comes a message. That message speaks to what we're like, what God is like to us and what our life is all about. And that message is almost always a lie! But we deeply believe it. We don't talk about it. We don't process it with a rational mind. We simply believe it. And it helps form not only our belief system, but it helps shape how we think about ourselves, how we view life and even how we think about God.

We have all suffered traumatic experiences. We all have been wounded, some more than others. You are who you are because those life experiences help shape how you think about yourself. Over the years, the structure of your self-concept forms which is comprised of the conclusions you have reached about yourself. If those conclusions are based on the truth of God's Word and an understanding of who He has made you to be, you are able to live in freedom with a world of possibilities before you. If, on the other hand, your self-concept is based on lies produced by negative life experiences, your self-concept can become a spiritual stronghold that blinds you to the truth and robs you of all that God intends.

The Grasshopper Syndrome

The book of Joshua chronicles the nation of Israel as she entered the Promised Land. After forty-plus years in the wilderness, the children of Israel finally crossed the Jordan River and began to inhabit the land that God had promised them all those years ago. It is a story that illustrates God's faithfulness to His people. I am convinced, however, that the significance of this story is as relevant to us today as it was to the Israelites then. In order to understand that significance, we must first understand the historical context that led to this turning point in the history of Israel.

Genesis recounts the triumphant story of Joseph as he went from an Egyptian prison to becoming second only to Pharaoh. Subsequently, Pharaoh invited Joseph's family to live in the choicest land of Egypt as thanks for Joseph's accomplishment of keeping Egypt from being ravaged by famine. Joseph's brothers, the sons of Israel, subsequently sought refuge in Egypt, and with each passing generation, their numbers multiplied and grew in strength.

Years later, however, a new pharaoh rose to power. He recognized that the Israelites were a strong and productive people and that the favor of God was upon them. He also knew that they had been given control over the best land in Egypt, land that produced the food supply for much of the nation. While the children of Israel had originally numbered seventy, they had grown to over a million by the time of the Exodus. Fearing they would someday choose to rebel against Egyptian rule and perhaps even seek to overthrow the government, the new pharaoh broke covenant with the Israelites and forced them into slavery. For 430 years, the Hebrews lived in Egypt, suffering for most of that period under the bondage of slavery under Pharaoh.

The Hebrews had become a threat to Pharaoh and his kingdom. He was aware of how powerful they were. His strategy, therefore, was to overpower them with fear, and he quickly appointed taskmasters over them. These taskmasters intimidated the Israelites with oppression and harassment, rendering them completely vulnerable to Egyptian control. Although the entire story of Israel in Egypt is full of great spiritual significance, one insight is of particular interest:

Pharaoh's goal was to keep the Hebrews from understanding their potential and who God had made them to be.

Things have not changed much over the centuries, have they? The enemy of God's people, along with his kingdom of darkness, utilizes that same strategy today—mainly because it is so successful! Our adversary still seeks to intimidate, harass and oppress with the same goals in mind: to keep God's people from knowing who they really are in Christ, to blind them from their potential and to keep them locked tight in the darkened cells of inferiority and despair.

In the book of Exodus, we see God answer the prayers of His people. Moses arose and led the children of Israel out of bondage. They experienced tremendous miracles by the hand of God on their behalf: the plagues against Egypt, the parting of the Red Sea, the pillar of fire and the cloud that led them by night and day, the manna from heaven, the water springing out of a rock—the list goes on and on. These were people who had seen the explicit, raw power of God.

In Numbers 13, the Israelites were in the wilderness, preparing to enter the Promised Land. They sent out twelve spies in order to scout out and survey the land and determine what they might encounter there. The spies returned and reported that, indeed, the land was flowing with milk and honey. The Promised Land was everything they could possibly want. It was, without a doubt, the place God had said it would be. But only two of the spies declared that it was theirs for the taking. The other ten gave an entirely different account.

> Then Caleb quieted the people before Moses and said, "We should by all means go up and take possession of it, for we shall surely overcome it." But the men who had gone up with him said, "We are not able to go up against the people, for they are too strong for us." So they gave out to the sons of Israel a bad report of the land which they had spied out, saying, "The land through which we have gone, in spying it out, is a land

that devours its inhabitants; and all the people whom we saw
in it are men of great size. There also we saw the Nephilim (the
sons of Anak are part of the Nephilim); and we became like
grasshoppers in our own sight, and so we were in their sight."

Numbers 13:30–33

The children of Israel, who had witnessed the raw and explicit
power of God moving on their behalf, perceived themselves
as nothing more than grasshoppers, unable to conquer or
inhabit the land God had promised them. They lost their
perspective on who they were, and subsequently, they lost
their right perspective of God.

In light of all the Israelites had witnessed before—the
powerful miracles, their deliverance from slavery, God's
provision in the wilderness—I do not believe they ques-
tioned whether God was powerful enough to defeat the
inhabitants of the Promised Land. They had watched God
split the Red Sea before them. In fact, they had walked
through the middle of the Red Sea on dry ground. They had
been active participants in God's miraculous work, and they
knew God could do anything. What they had difficulty
believing was not God's ability to perform miracles, but
whether God would perform His miracles *through them.*

Up to that time, the Israelites had witnessed God move on
their behalf, either through His own sovereign act (such as
raining manna from heaven) or through Moses acting in
faith and obedience. Now, however, their own faith and
obedience became essential—although God still promised to
go before them and drive out the inhabitants of the land.
The land had been given to them generations before, but
they would now have to go in and take possession over it.

As they faced this challenge, the potential fulfillment of
their national dream, they could have easily recalled all the
miracles that had brought them to this point. How awesome
was their God! They were His people, full of purpose and

destiny! Yes, there were obstacles. Yes, there were huge challenges—but they were God's people! That was their identity, and God had chosen to accomplish His mighty work through them.

In my opinion, the words found in Numbers 13:33 are among the most tragic you will ever read, and yet they are so descriptive of the human condition: "We became like grasshoppers in our own sight, and so we were in their sight." The children of Israel became paralyzed by their negative self-concept. They saw themselves as insignificant grasshoppers, even though they had witnessed the most outstanding miracles in history. Even though the love and grace of God had delivered them from the hands of cruel taskmasters, slavery had still left its mark upon their identity. They were, indeed, God's chosen people, but their self-concept remained locked up in Egypt, where they were still slaves, grasshoppers in their own sight.

"We are not able to go up against the people. They are too strong for us," are words of utter defeat and paralyzed potential. And for the next forty years, the Israelites wandered in the wilderness, going around the same old mountain only God knows how many times.

Do not be mistaken. The wilderness wandering did not mean that God had forsaken them. They were still His people. He continued to care for, lead, watch over and provide for them in the wilderness because of His deep love for them. He never forsakes those who are His own. Nevertheless, that generation never entered nor possessed the land God had promised them. Their dream never became a reality. They were so close, and yet so very far away!

The children of Israel saw themselves as grasshoppers even though they were the chosen people of God, created in His image with purpose and destiny. The "grasshopper syndrome"—their slave mentality and crippled self-image— kept them from taking the land God had promised them.

"We are not able to go up against the people, for they are too strong for us."

All of us have internal guiding pictures of ourselves. These self-portraits have been painted in the heat of life experiences and developed by the things we deeply believe about who we are. It is out of these self-portraits that we build relationships, make decisions and choose careers. In fact, every aspect of our lives is governed by how we see ourselves. If your inner self-portrait is distorted or damaged, it can lock you up for years and keep you from experiencing the blessing God intended for you from the beginning. If, on the other hand, you maintain a right self-portrait, it can empower you to pursue and realize all of the healing, confidence, purpose and joy God so desires to bring into your life.

Chapter 2

It Was Meant to Be So Different

There was our little girl, on stage, in the spotlight, ready for her solo. All eyes in the audience were fixed on her. This was her big moment.

Palms were sweaty. Hearts beat fast. Hands involuntarily trembled. Of course, I am referring to my wife and me. Our daughter Debbie was fine. She had never showed an ounce of interest in singing, at least not in front of a group of people. Yet there she was, standing on stage in front of hundreds of people, about to sing a solo for her kindergarten graduation program.

Debbie appeared to have all the confidence in the world— as if she had been doing this all her life. On the other hand, my wife, Bev, and I were absolute wrecks. Images of Debbie freezing up just as she opened her mouth to sing, or becoming paralyzed with stage fright, raced through our minds. What would happen if she ran off the stage in tears or discovered that she couldn't sing? Events like that could scar a kid for life.

While Bev and I sunk deeper into our seats, our stomachs knotting up, praying that God would protect Debbie from all of our fears, she walked to the front of her class, grabbed the microphone like a pro and began to sing. Out of her mouth came the most powerful voice, singing, "I am a promise!

I am a possibility! I am a great big bundle of PO-tentiality! I can be anything—anything God wants me to be!"

I was amazed that a voice that big could come from such a tiny body. With every line our daughter sang, Bev and I sat up in our seats a little higher. Before long, we were nudging one another as if to say, "That's our daughter up there! We knew all along she could do it!"

As Debbie continued to sing, two lines from her song kept going through my mind: "I am a great big bundle of potentiality! I can be anything God wants me to be." As I looked into her face, it became so clear. God had given Debbie all the ability she needed to become everything He intended her to be. Debbie, as all of us are at that young age, was a bundle of potential—a gift filled with possibilities and dreams, talents and abilities, all eagerly waiting to be unwrapped.

Nevertheless, as I continued to watch her perform, I also became painfully aware that if hell had its way, all of Debbie's potential would remain unrealized, her talent and ability paralyzed by the circumstances of life. Indeed, if hell's destructive plan were to be successful, all the dreams of her young heart would go unfulfilled. I had seen it happen all too often in the lives of so many others. I had even experienced its devastating effects in my own life.

As I looked into the faces of the kids standing around Debbie, I could not help but wonder what life would have been like if man had remained in the Garden of Eden. How different would we be if Adam and Eve had not fallen prey to the serpent's deception—that man could find significance apart from God (see Genesis 3:5)?

From generation to generation, the questions remain the same: Who am I? What is life all about? Man's quest for significance never ends. Unfortunately, we look in all the wrong places to recapture the fulfillment God intended from the beginning. There is an unquenched thirst deep within all of us—a deep knowledge that it was all meant to be so different.

It Was Meant to Be So Different

I fail to remember when or where I first heard it. I do remember that it always seemed to be an accepted fact, at least in my mind. It was one of those things you always knew but were never quite sure why it was true or where it came from. In fact, I assumed it was in the Bible! It was the idea that God created man primarily for fellowship with Himself. In my mind, the story went something like this: After God created the heavens and the earth with everything in them, something was still lacking. Realizing how lonely He was and that His creation could not completely fulfill Him, He decided to create something more like Himself, someone to be with, to talk to. Therefore, God conjured up creatures made in His likeness—people fashioned in His image to ensure He would have friends to fill out the balance of His creation.

While God has, from the beginning, both desired and sought out fellowship with man, this is only a fraction of His intended purpose for humanity. From the beginning, the Bible boldly declares that God's primary purpose for the creation of man was not so much *fellowship* as it was *rulership*.

> Then God said, "Let Us make man in Our image, according to Our likeness; and let them rule over the fish of the sea and over the birds of the air and over the cattle and over all the earth, and over every creeping thing that creeps on the earth."
>
> Genesis 1:26

From the beginning, God has invited man into "partnership" with Himself. This was, for me, a new revelation. God's intended purpose, while certainly including a relationship with man, went far beyond the desire just to have someone to talk to. He intended partnership with man in ruling over and caring for the earth, His creation.

The opening pages of Scripture set the stage for an understanding of God's intended role for man, as well as the tragedy that follows.

Like most pastors, I am always looking for sermon material. Every book, magazine, television program and even the latest pop song are sermons in the making. While I was sitting in the waiting room of my doctor's office one day, the cover of a current psychology magazine caught my attention. The entire issue was dedicated to the subject of self-image and personal value. As I quickly scanned the collection of articles, I came across one written by a psychiatrist who was laying out the requirements for living a successful, fulfilled life.

Nothing that the man said gave me any indication that he understood the biblical story of man's creation, nor did I get the impression that he was a follower of Jesus. But what intrigued me was that the qualities listed by this psychiatrist as being necessary for personal fulfillment were the same qualities given by God to man at creation.

The psychiatrist wrote about the importance of understanding your identity, to know who you are and be comfortable with it. He also examined the necessity of empowerment, to have an area of your life in which you are master, commander-in-chief or boss. In other words, we all need a realm of authority in which we make decisions on how things should be. With that authority comes responsibility, not only for the outcome of those decisions, but also for the environment in which we function.

As I read further, I found it interesting that the psychiatrist addressed the importance of people connecting with one another: People cannot live meaningful lives in isolation. Significant relationships are at the core of human fulfillment.

Although he did not talk about spiritual life in Christian terms, such as a "relationship with God" or a "personal experience with Jesus Christ," he did emphasize the necessity of spiritual understanding, that we are spiritual beings and must relate to a greater power beyond ourselves.

As you read the Genesis account of creation, you will quickly discover that these are the same qualities God intended for His creation from the beginning.

Identity

Let Us make man in Our image, according to Our likeness.

Genesis 1:26

While being created in the image of God has nothing to do with our physical appearance, it does mean that we were created:

- With a capacity to know God and relate to Him intimately
- With a sovereign free will to make moral choices
- With a mind, a will and emotions
- With the potential for everlasting life

Authority

Let them rule [or have authority] . . . over all the earth.

Genesis 1:26

God's plan for His creation included partnership between man and Himself in ruling the earth. In reality, we were created to be in a type of co-regency, at least as far as the earth was concerned. God was to remain ruler of the entire universe. To man, He delegated authority of the affairs of earth.

Responsibility

> God blessed them; and God said to them, "Be fruitful and multiply, and fill the earth, and subdue it."
>
> Genesis 1:28

There is a tremendous sense of excitement on the part of God toward mankind illustrated in this verse. God was delighted with mankind and put His blessing upon them. In fact, He was so pleased, He directed man to reproduce and create other human beings.

God also set in motion man's responsibility to care for the earth and all of His creation therein. Man was meant to nurture the earth, to watch over it and ensure that things remained in proper balance. In this way, mankind would reap the benefits of all God had created. With this twofold initiative, to reproduce and to benefit from God's creation, man's responsibility was therefore established.

Companionship

> Then the LORD God said, "It is not good for the man to be alone; I will make him a helper suitable for him."
>
> Genesis 2:18

> The man said,
>   "This is now bone of my bones,
>   And flesh of my flesh."
>
> Genesis 2:23

You may have heard the old quote, "No man is an island." Indeed, God immediately addressed the issue of loneliness, the most devastating plague that has ever swept the planet.

Relationship with Himself

> They heard the sound of the LORD God walking in the garden in the cool of the day.
>
> Genesis 3:8

God gave the man and woman everything they needed for fulfillment, as well as everything required to fulfill their destiny and the plan God intended for them to achieve.

Tragedy in Paradise

Scripture does not clearly record how long the man and woman lived in the fullness of God's intended purpose. It does tell us that when Adam and Eve chose to listen to the voice of the deceiver and violate the one condition set by God—"but from the tree of the knowledge of good and evil you shall not eat, for in the day that you eat from it you will surely die" (Genesis 2:17)—tragedy struck.

In a moment of time, man—who had been given complete fulfillment, broad authority, personal significance, awesome gifting and amazing potential—was plunged into the depths of despair and brokenness. His identity, while still reflecting the image of the Creator, had now been infected with sin.

With the entrance of sin into the world, man's identity became confused. Questions like, "Who am I?" "What is my value?" "Where do I belong?" and "What is my purpose?"—although certainly important for each of us to answer—are a reflection of the turmoil introduced by sin. Man, who had been created with identity and purpose, now searches for significance apart from the God who gave him life, value and the promise of fulfilled potential.

The first verses of Genesis 5 contain one of the most tragic pictures in human history. As you read, pay close attention to the third verse:

> This is the book of the generations of Adam. In the day when God created man, He made him in the likeness of God. He created them male and female, and He blessed them and named them Man in the day when they were created. When

Adam had lived one hundred and thirty years, he became the
father of a son in his own likeness, according to his image, and
named him Seth.

Genesis 5:1–3

Did you see that? Adam, who had been created in the image
of God, was able to create in his own likeness and image! As
a result, from generation to generation, not only is the image
of God passed on, but so, too, is the confusion and distortion
of man's broken image.

The source of our identity crises is our alienation from
God, who gave mankind identity in the first place. But
people continue to search for significance apart from their
Creator, obsessed with finding reason and purpose on their
own. However, apart from God, we will never understand or
successfully address the root cause of our inner turmoil.

All that was intended for man's fulfillment—identity,
authority, responsibility, companionship and relationship
with God Himself—was significantly affected by man's choice
to disobey God's command. Subsequently, man's identity
became confused by sin. His authority was relinquished to
the kingdom of darkness. His role changed from one of
partnership with God in ruling over the earth to being subject
to the earth itself.

Furthermore, man and woman, devastated by their loss of
identity, began a lifelong struggle to find a place of significance. Their prior companionship degraded into a power
struggle with each grasping for a position of control over the
other.

The Genesis 3 account of Adam and Eve in their final
moments in the Garden is heartbreaking. Yet there is also
an element of possible redemption. God brought man face
to face with the consequences of sin, while giving him a
glimpse at God's plan for salvation. God makes the first
promise regarding a Redeemer (see Genesis 3:15), and it

introduced hope in the midst of hopelessness. God also hinted of the sacrifice that would have to be made to provide covering for man's sin (see Genesis 3:21).

After bringing mankind face to face with the consequences of his sin, God was forced to expel them from the Garden. For years, I pictured God doing this in a fit of anger (justified though it would have been), wielding a whip in the midst of righteous fury. But I have come to realize that, while God is angry at sin and how it violates His righteous character as well as devastates His creation, He still deeply loves people, and He always will! Instead of God driving Adam and Eve out of the Garden in anger, He drove them out in tears, with a heart that was broken.

We have all visited places we will never forget. Whether it be historical landmarks or cities of renown, they are forever etched in our minds. The day Bev and I visited Dachau was one of those times for me. It was a summer day, yet there was a light drizzle when we drove into what appeared to be a beautiful German village just outside the city of Munich. In my mind, Dachau was a place of horror. It was hard to believe that some of the greatest atrocities in human history had taken place in such a quaint, picturesque landscape.

As we walked through the entrance gate to what had once been one of the infamous death camps of the Third Reich, a blanket of silence seemed to fall over us. Our first stop was the museum building and a display of photographs that documented the tremendous pain and suffering experienced by those in the camp at the hands of the Nazis. After just a few brief moments, Bev and I had seen far more than we wanted to. Some of those pictures I still wish I could forget, although I know I never will.

We moved out of the museum to cross the center court-yard where the barracks had once been located. Toward the back of the camp were monuments honoring those who had lost their lives at Dachau. To the right of the monuments was the exact place where tens of thousands had been slaughtered. We continued to walk across the courtyard in absolute silence. As a soft rain began to fall, I remember whispering to Bev, "It's almost as though God were crying."

In fact, I believe God did weep over the atrocities of Dachau. This was not what He intended for His creation. Places like Dachau and Auschwitz, My Lai, Uganda, Jonestown, Kosovo, Columbine, the World Trade Center in New York City and countless other sites of infamous slaughters were never in God's plan for mankind. They are the result of man's sin. The AIDS epidemic that has ravaged and destroyed millions on every continent, as well as other terrifying diseases such as Ebola, E. Coli and viral strains that are immune to antibiotics are the result of sin's destructive presence—as is racism, sexism, hatred, bigotry, fear, crime and any other examples of man's inhumanity to man. This is not what God originally intended for all of us. It was meant to be so different!

Starting Over!

> For God so loved the world, that He gave His only begotten Son, that whoever believes in Him shall not perish, but have eternal life. For God did not send the Son into the world to judge the world, but that the world might be saved through Him.
>
> John 3:16–17

Have you ever wished that you could start your life all over again? Maybe even assume a new identity? Most of us do at one time or another. Perhaps you have said to yourself, *If only I could erase the past, with all of my mistakes and failures! If I could just start over with a clean slate, it would be so different!*

Ah, but that would be too good to be true, right? That's impossible. No one can get a second chance at life—or can we?

In reality, that is exactly the message Jesus came to bring! Starting over—it is His message of hope. You *can* start over again! And He is the One who can make it possible!

The devastation of man's sin is so great that it cannot be easily fixed or cleaned up. The destruction at the core of man's being—his identity—is so deep and thorough, only an act of the sovereign Creator's grace and mercy could possibly bring restoration. But because of God's determination to restore His original destiny for mankind, He initiated His plan of redemption—even before man left the Garden. His plan was as follows:

- In the presence of fallen man in the Garden, the Father set forth both a promise and the provision for mankind's redemption (see Genesis 3:15, 21).

- Throughout the Old Testament, the Father continued to unfold His redemptive plan: first, in relationship to a man (Abraham), then to a family (the sons of Israel) and finally to an entire nation (Israel). The Law was given to bring man face to face with his inability to achieve righteousness apart from God. Through the prophets, He pointed to the coming Messiah, God's ultimate Promise and Provision.

- At the appointed time, God sent His Son, Jesus (Emmanuel—"God with us"), with a message of hope: reconciling God and man through His own blood shed on the cross (see Colossians 1:20) and restoring man to his intended place of partnership with his Creator (see 2 Corinthians 5:18–19; Galatians 3:24; 4:4).

- The cross of Christ becomes a place of exchange. We exchange our unrighteousness for His righteousness, our rejection for His acceptance, our old fallen identity for His new identity.

- When we put our faith and trust in the work of Christ on the cross at Calvary, we become a new creation. From that moment on, God sees us "in Christ." We have a new identity. We are accepted before the Father because we are now "in Christ" (2 Corinthians 5:17).

"Therefore if anyone is in Christ, he is a new creature; the old things passed away; behold, new things have come" (2 Corinthians 5:17).

Through God's plan of redemption in Jesus Christ and our act of receiving Jesus as our Savior, the original qualities God had instilled within mankind at creation become restored, overturning the devastating effects of sin. We are able to start over!

Man's Significance to God

Throughout the Bible, it is clear that God places tremendous significance upon mankind. C. S. Lewis, one of the great twentieth-century Christian writers, believed the most important thing about a man was how God saw him. In fact, the first step in establishing a healthy self-concept is to understand what God the Father truly thinks about you.

In the first chapter of Genesis, it is clear that God is the center of the universe. Everything came into being as a result of His Word, including mankind. However, in a very real sense, man is at the center of God's love and affection because he is the only being created in His image (see Genesis 1:26–27). It can be said, therefore, that man is the pinnacle of God's creative efforts.

Subsequently, each person has the potential of becoming a child of God (see John 1:12–13). This cannot be said of any other created being, including angels. God values us so much that He has dispatched His ministering hosts to protect us. Angels have been commissioned to watch over human beings (see Psalm 91:11–12; Hebrews 1:14).

Man is also the object of God's redemptive work (see John 3:16). Again, redemption is not available to the angels. The Bible describes how a third of the angels in heaven fell when Satan rebelled. There is, however, no biblical plan of redemption for those angels. Nevertheless, as a result of the cross, there is a plan of redemption for you and me. Indeed, if man were not significant to God, would He have sacrificed Himself for our salvation?

Mankind was worth the supreme sacrifice of God (see 1 Corinthians 6:20; 1 Peter 1:18–19). The value of gold is based not on its own inherent quality, but on the fact that people will pay such a high price for it. The consumer sets the price. From God's point of view, if we were to have a price tag placed on our lives, we are worth the blood of His Son, Jesus Christ. That being the case, we could not be of more significant value to God.

God has been made rich because we, who are Christ's, have been given to Him (see Ephesians 1:18). We often think the opposite is true—that we have been made rich because of all that Jesus has done for us, which is absolutely correct. But on the other hand, because Jesus paid for us with His life, and we have been redeemed back to God, God has also been made rich. The cross illustrates just how valuable we are to God. We are His treasures!

Once we have become believers, Jesus Himself prepares a place for us to dwell with Him in eternity (see John 14:1–3). We often think of how exciting it will be to enter heaven and dwell with Christ forever. But have you ever considered the fact that Jesus is equally as excited by the prospect of spending eternity with us?

C. S. Lewis was right. Understanding how significant we are to God is of foundational importance. On the other hand, another great twentieth-century Christian writer,

A. W. Tozer, believed that the most important thing about you was how you thought about God. I feel that both sentiments carry equal weight, although I would go so far as to add a third. How you see yourself can have as much of an impact upon your life as how you see God and how you believe God sees you. If you are able to place these three aspects into right perspective in your life, you will realize just how much you mean to God and how much He desires to see your purpose fulfilled. Some people can accomplish this without difficulty, but for many of us, it can be an intimidating process. It requires you to deal with aspects of your life where you may have been deeply wounded. My hope is that as you read further, you will allow the Holy Spirit free reign to redeem your life. If you do, you truly will never be the same.

Chapter 3

Who Do You Think You Are?

Without question, next to Jesus, Peter is my favorite New Testament personality. Peter is so colorful, so spontaneous and opinionated. There was never a boring minute when he was around. Furthermore, he did so many dumb things! Paul was brilliant. John was prophetic. But Peter was all too human. I can really relate to him.

One example comes to mind: When the soldiers came to arrest Jesus in the Garden of Gethsemane, Peter whipped out his sword and, in a moment of impulse, cut off the ear of the high priest's servant! I have always wondered, why the servant? Why not go after the soldier who was taking Jesus into custody—or the high priest himself? And why cut off his ear? Why not go for the throat? Or, really, why do it at all?

Another story involves Peter and the disciples on the Sea of Galilee. There they were, sailing peacefully across the waters, when a sudden, violent storm arose, causing the sea to pound against the side of their little boat. The Scriptures say that somewhere between 3:00 and 6:00 A.M., the darkest hours of the night, Jesus came to them walking on the sea. While the other disciples reacted in fear, Peter called out, "Lord, if that's You, bid me to come to You on the water!"

Was he serious?! Perhaps it was impulse mixed with a little faith that made Peter blurt out such a strange request.

Nevertheless, the moment Jesus heard Peter's response, He said to him, "Okay, Peter, it's Me! Come on out here!" Without hesitation, Peter jumped out of the boat and began walking on the sea. That is, until he realized exactly what he was doing and began to sink.

Do you see what I mean? Peter is so easy to relate to! The more I know about Peter, the more I love him. Peter's life message seems to be, "If God can transform my life and make something great out of it, He can do the same with yours. If He can change my identity (and that is exactly what God did), He can change yours as well."

From the moment Peter first encountered Jesus, after his brother Andrew brought him to meet the Messiah, it became obvious that God had planned for Peter to become something more than he himself had ever dreamed possible. The village fisherman was to become a fisher of men. The ordinary Simon, with all of his insecurities and weaknesses, all of his human fumblings and blunders, would become an extra-ordinary apostle—the Rock! Jesus saw something in Simon Peter that perhaps no one else would ever have seen. He saw what Peter would become.

Later on, Jesus stood with His disciples on a hillside at Caesarea Philippi, a city dominated not only by the gods of the ancient world but by man's dream for power, position and authority. Surrounding this city, on the slopes of Mount Hermon in northern Israel, were no less than fourteen temples of Baal, the Syrian god of productivity and pros-perity. On the side of the mountain, dazzling in the sun for all to see, was a white marble temple built by Herod the Great and dedicated to the Roman Caesar. It was, in fact, a monument to man's ambition and world domination.

Overlooking the city from high on an adjacent hill was a cave where the mythological Greek god Pan was said to have lived. Pan was the half-man, half-goat god of nature from whose name we derive modern *pantheism*, the belief that god can be found in "all" or in everything. Greeks believed that Pan had the ability to fill people and animals with sudden terror; the word *panic* comes from his name.

In the same cave is a deep reservoir of water that is fed by a natural spring. This is the key source of the Jordan River. By Jesus's day, the Jordan River had become all but sacred to the devout Jews, whose religious practices had become filled with tradition and self-righteousness.

It is an incredibly powerful picture! In an atmosphere dominated by ancient pagan religion, the powers of darkness and the pride of men, where fear, greed, self-righteousness, human might and authority ruled with colossal strength, Jesus asked the most defining question in history: "Who do people say that I am?" (Matthew 16:13).

And as if that were not enough, He pressed the issue even further, asking His disciples, "Who do *you* say that I am?" (Matthew 16:15, emphasis mine).

Peter, who had just had a revelation of who this Galilean carpenter really was, spoke revolutionary words and thereby framed the heart of the Christian Church: "You are the Christ, the Son of the living God!" (Matthew 16:16).

In other words, Peter was saying, "You're the One we've been looking for! You're the Anointed One, the Messiah! It's You!"

Impulsiveness is not always a negative trait. In this case, Peter's impulsiveness was right on. He had a revelation of Jesus. Something happened deep inside him, and he would never be the same. Then Jesus responded to Peter's declaration with further revelation:

> Jesus said to him, "Blessed are you, Simon Barjona, because flesh and blood did not reveal this to you, but My Father who is in heaven. I also say to you that you are Peter, and upon this rock I will build My church; and the gates of Hades will not overpower it."
>
> Matthew 16:17–18

This passage of Scripture is crucial! The message of Jesus's words here is so critical to the way you live your life, as well as to your fulfillment and ministry, that you cannot afford to miss it! At the risk of sounding redundant, allow me to paraphrase Jesus's response:

"Peter, the Father has given you a revelation of who I am. You didn't see this on your own. It came by divine revelation. Now, with that understanding and with that same spirit of revelation, let Me show you who I have made you to be. I want you to understand your new identity and what it means. Then I am going to take you and others like you— ordinary people who have had a revelation of who I am and who begin to understand who I have made them to be—and build a Church so powerful that all the authority of hell cannot overpower it!"

I am so glad it was Peter to whom Jesus was speaking in this passage because of how easily I can relate to him. If God could do something so significant in Peter, there is hope for me! And that is the message behind this book. It is a message I want you to receive loud and clear: *There is hope for you!*

God begins His work in our lives by changing our identity. Through Jesus, we have new life—not just another way to fix up our old lives or make what is dysfunctional, functional. The bold proclamation of 2 Corinthians 5:17, "If anyone is in Christ, *he is a new creature*" (emphasis mine), is at the heart of the Gospel message. When you receive Jesus as your Savior, you have new life and a new identity!

All the same, there is a world of difference between having a new identity and actually seeing yourself differently. Most of us continue to live out an old, broken picture of ourselves long after our identity has been changed by Jesus. Because the old picture is often built on the lies we believe about ourselves, we continue to live in defeat or, at best, mediocrity far beneath God's intended purpose for our lives; a purpose that includes both our personal fulfillment and our ability to make a difference in a desperately needy world.

The issue was clearly settled that day at Caesarea Philippi when Jesus responded to Peter's declaration of His identity. Jesus's response, however, did not stop with Peter on that hillside. He continues to respond to each of us today—right now He is saying, "You have had a revelation of who I am. Now let Me show you who you are and who I have created you to be." As He did with Peter, so He will do with you, "and all the powers of hell will not conquer it!" (Matthew 16:18, NLT).

What Does It Mean to Be "In Christ"?

When you become a believer in Jesus Christ, the Scriptures say you become a new creation. You have a new identity. From that moment on, the Father identifies you with His Son, Jesus. He sees you "in Christ" (Galatians 2:20; Ephesians 1:1–14; Colossians 3:1–3).

1. You are a new creation.

> Therefore if anyone is in Christ, he is a new creature; the old things passed away; behold, new things have come.
>
> 2 Corinthians 5:17

2. You are a child of God.

> But as many as received Him, to them He gave the right to become children of God, even to those who believe in His name.
>
> John 1:12

3. All your sins are forgiven.

> And you, being dead in your trespasses and the uncircumcision of your flesh, He has made alive together with Him,

having forgiven you all trespasses, having wiped out the handwriting of requirements that was against us, which was contrary to us. And He has taken it out of the way, having nailed it to the cross.

Colossians 2:13–14, NKJV

4. You have received eternal life.

Most assuredly, I say to you, he who hears My word and believes in Him who sent Me has everlasting life, and shall not come into judgment, but has passed from death into life.

John 5:24, NKJV

5. You have been delivered from the kingdom of darkness and transferred into the Kingdom of God.

He has delivered us from the power of darkness and conveyed us into the kingdom of the Son of His love, in whom we have redemption through His blood, the forgiveness of sins.

Colossians 1:13–14, NKJV

6. Christ lives in you through the power of the Holy Spirit.

To them God willed to make known what are the riches of the glory of this mystery among the Gentiles: which is Christ in you, the hope of glory.

Colossians 1:27, NKJV

7. You are declared righteous.

For He made Him who knew no sin to be sin for us, that we might become the righteousness of God in Him.

2 Corinthians 5:21, NKJV

8. You are absolutely accepted by God.

For it pleased the Father that in Him all the fullness should dwell, and by Him to reconcile all things to Himself, by Him, whether things on earth or things in heaven, having made peace through the blood of His cross. And you, who once were alienated and enemies in your mind by wicked works, yet now He has reconciled in the body of His flesh through death, to present you holy, and blameless, and above reproach in His sight.

Colossians 1:19–22, NKJV

9. You belong to God.

Or do you not know that your body is the temple of the Holy Spirit who is in you, whom you have from God, and you are not your own? For you were bought at a price; therefore glorify God in your body and in your spirit, which are God's.

1 Corinthians 6:19–20, NKJV

10. The Holy Spirit begins the process of conforming you into the image of Christ.

Beloved, now we are children of God; and it has not yet been revealed what we shall be, but we know that when He is revealed, we shall be like Him, for we shall see Him as He is.

1 John 3:2, NKJV

11. You enter into a love relationship with God.

In this the love of God was manifested toward us, that God has sent His only begotten Son into the world, that we might live through Him. In this is love, not that we loved God, but that He loved us and sent His Son to be the propitiation for our sins. Beloved, if God so loved us, we also ought to love one another.

1 John 4:9–11, NKJV

You are now a new creature in Jesus Christ. That is the most important fact about your identity, and it is the basis of understanding who you are. This is not something you have to psych yourself up for or talk yourself into. It is the truth, period!

Old Words with Radical Meanings

There are a number of old theological terms used by pastors and teachers over the years that I call "church words," words that have little meaning to most people today. Some of these words are a bit difficult to pronounce, *propitiation*, for example. But even if you could pronounce it clearly, you might wonder what *propitiation* means and what it has to do with you and your identity. Indeed, while these words certainly seem antiquated and can sound so religious, they still have significant meanings and can be very powerful. When correctly understood, they have the ability to radically affect your life. Before we look at these words more carefully, allow me to clarify a couple of important points that can help you grasp just how significant the following terms are.

1. Even though these are theological terms, they have very practical meanings that apply to our daily lives. Therefore I have limited the definitions of these terms to the subject at hand. I want to lay a foundation on which an accurate understanding of our new identity in Christ can be built. It is not my intention to explore the depth of meaning found in each word, nor is it my purpose to exhaust a point of theology.

2. For us to begin to understand God's response to man's sin, it is necessary that we understand two things about His character: First, He is always and in everything righteous and holy; and second, He deeply loves people (see John 3:16).

With these two things in mind, let us look at how God responds to man's sin, and on that basis, define these very important words.

Many of us find it difficult to clarify how a loving God could pronounce judgment on sinful men. If He really loved them, could He not just overlook their transgression? Perhaps He could just give them a stern lecture or make them stand in the corner or something. Then afterward, in His love and mercy, maybe He could give them another chance. After all, we all deserve a second chance—right?

The truth is, man's sin was not only a deep violation of God's righteous character, but it also broke His relationship with the people that He loved, bringing destruction and death where He intended life. Sin's effect is so devastating, its pollution and bondage so thorough and its consequences so far-reaching that the only right and just response from a righteous, holy and loving God is judgment and wrath. The Scriptures indicate that there is only one penalty for sin.

> The person who sins will die.
>
> Ezekiel 18:20

> But from the tree of the knowledge of good and evil you shall not eat, for in the day that you eat from it you will surely die.
>
> Genesis 2:17

> For the wages of sin is death.
>
> Romans 6:23

To satisfy both His righteous character and His deep love for mankind, but knowing that man was unable to restore the relationship, God Himself provided the solution. He sent His own Son as a substitute to take man's place in judgment and death. Jesus took upon Himself the righteous wrath of God, the wrath that mankind rightly deserved.

Propitiation

> In this the love of God was manifested toward us, that God has sent His only begotten Son into the world, that we might

live through Him. In this is love, not that we loved God, but
that He loved us and sent His Son to be the propitiation for
our sins.

1 John 4:9–10, NKJV

Did you notice the word *propitiation* in these verses? Regarding
your identity in Christ, *propitiation* means that the punish-
ment you deserved because of your sin and rebellion, Jesus
has taken for you. Because of His sacrifice on the cross in your
place, the righteousness of God, which demanded that the
penalty for sin be fully paid, has been satisfied. When you
put your faith and trust in Jesus and in the power of His
sacrifice, you appropriate upon yourself all that He has done
on your behalf.

> ► **In Christ I am loved. There is no fear of punishment.
> Jesus took the punishment that I deserved so that I
> could freely receive all of God's love and grace.**

Reconciliation

The subject of reconciliation is quite a popular one these
days. Much is being said and written about it. Throughout
the years, I have been involved in an important ministry
founded by a good friend of mine, John Dawson. His
organization, the International Reconciliation Coalition, is
dedicated to facilitating reconciliation between nations,
ethnicities and other groups of people who have historically
been at odds with one another for years.

Even so, while reconciliation between people and nations
reflects the heart of God and should be part of our lifestyle,
man's greatest need is reconciliation with God Himself.
Without that ultimate reconciliation, all other attempts,
while they may have some measure of success, will fall far
short of the desired goal.

But God demonstrates His own love toward us, in that while we were yet sinners, Christ died for us. Much more then, having now been justified by His blood, we shall be saved from the wrath of God through Him. For if while we were enemies we were reconciled to God through the death of His Son, much more, having been reconciled, we shall be saved by His life. And not only this, but we also exult in God through our Lord Jesus Christ, through whom we have now received the reconciliation.

Romans 5:8–11

Reconciliation means that those who were enemies have become friends. Their relationship is restored. Where there once was rejection and alienation, there is now love and total acceptance. Where sin once made us unworthy and unacceptable before God, the blood of Jesus Christ has reconciled us to God. In Christ, you are as acceptable before God as is His Son, Jesus.

Do you realize how exciting this is? If you have ever struggled with rejection, it can be a joyful revelation!

▶ **On the cross, Jesus took my rejection. In place of it, He gave me acceptance. I am as welcome in the presence of Father God as Jesus is, because I am in Christ.**

And you, who once were alienated and enemies in your mind by wicked works, yet now He has reconciled in the body of His flesh through death, to present you holy, and blameless, and above reproach in His sight.

Colossians 1:21–22, NKJV

Justification

I remember listening to a traveling evangelist when I was a boy as he spoke about justification. At that time, it seemed like a strange word. I clearly remember the man saying that from the moment you receive Jesus as Savior, God sees you "just as if" you had never sinned! "That's justification!" he exclaimed.

The evangelist asked us to picture a ledger. On one side all of your sins and bad deeds are listed; on the other side is the righteousness of Jesus. When you become a Christian, God makes an exchange. The page with all your sins written upon it is transferred to Jesus, and the page with His right- eousness is transferred to you. This is what justification by faith means. I have never forgotten that illustration, even though at the time I did not completely understand it.

Justification simply means that you have been completely forgiven. All of your sins—past, present and future, as well as the penalty for those sins—were paid for by Jesus on the cross. He took your sins and, in exchange, gave you His righteousness. "For He made Him who knew no sin to be sin for us, that we might become the righteousness of God in Him" (2 Corinthians 5:21, NKJV).

▶ **In Christ, I am completely forgiven, and because the righteousness of Christ has been transferred to me, I am pleasing to God.**

Regeneration

> Therefore, if anyone is in Christ, he is a new creation; old things have passed away; behold, all things have become new.
> 2 Corinthians 5:17, NKJV

The message of this verse describes exactly what regeneration is all about. It is not reformation—it is transformation. It is not a Christian self-help program in which you try to clean up the old—it is a whole new life.

Regeneration is really the heart of the Gospel. A psychol- ogist can help you think and feel better about yourself, but only God can regenerate you and make you a brand-new creature!

> ▶ **In Christ, I am a new creation! I have a new identity!**

Redemption

> In Him we have redemption through His blood, the forgiveness of sins; according to the riches of His grace.
>
> Ephesians 1:7, NKJV

> In whom we have redemption through His blood, the forgiveness of sins.
>
> Colossians 1:14, NKJV

The word *redemption* is often used in regard to purchasing a slave with his freedom in mind. Biblically, the word refers to one's deliverance from the power and control of sin, when you are transferred from the kingdom of darkness into the Kingdom of God.

> Stand fast therefore in the liberty by which Christ has made us free, and do not be entangled again with a yoke of bondage.
>
> Galatians 5:1, NKJV

> ▶ **In Christ, I have freedom from the power of sin. I am free to become everything God wants me to be.**

What Is the Difference between Identity and Self-Image?

Although the words *identity* and *self-image* are often used interchangeably, they are actually quite different. Identity is, in fact, who you are. When you receive Jesus, according to 2 Corinthians 5:17, you become a new creation. From that moment on, God sees you "in Christ"—a new person with a new identity.

Identity is fact. You may not always feel or think like a new creation, nor will you always act like a new creation. But the truth is that you are a new creation. It is your identity.

Your self-image, on the other hand, is how you see yourself. It is a mental picture composed of the conclusions you have reached about yourself, conclusions that are based on your life experiences and the opinions you form regarding those experiences.

How you see yourself is vital to how you live your life, how you build relationships and even how you relate to God. The tragedy is that many Christians fail to see themselves in truth. They are aware of their new identity, but they still think in terms of their old selves. As a result, they continue to live their lives the way they always have, allowing all of their past failures and suffering to dictate who they are and how they should act. Indeed, how you see yourself will govern how you live your life!

The best definition of a right self-image I have ever read is found in Psalm 139:13–14 (NKJV): "For You formed my inward parts; You covered me in my mother's womb. I will praise You, for I am fearfully and wonderfully made; Marvelous are Your works, And that my soul knows very well."

Allow me to paraphrase what I believe David was saying in this prayer of thanksgiving: "Father, You did a good job when You made me, and I love You for it!"

David was not boasting in his own ability or his own goodness. He was not saying, "Look at me! I am the greatest!" But neither was David putting himself down. He was acknowledging that God was his Creator and that He had done a wonderful job. It is a prayer of thankfulness that also reflects a healthy self-image.

I mentioned before that Peter is my favorite New Testament personality. In the Old Testament, my favorite is David. Like Peter, he seems so real and easy to relate to. The Bible does not portray David as perfect; in fact, it consistently exposes his humanness. As you read the psalms that David wrote, you encounter just about every human emotion—from anger and depression to extreme joy and elation. David experienced times of great affirmation as well as times of deep disappointment, both with himself and with those around him. He faced family challenges that shook his kingdom; he suffered from broken relationships, personal despair, the untimely deaths of those he deeply loved and severe chastisement for disobedience and rebellion.

Yet in all of this, he never seems preoccupied with himself. We see a confidence in David. He understood who God was and who God had made him to be. David was a man after God's own heart, with a strong, healthy and right sense of self.

Goals of a Right Self-Image

> I beseech you therefore, brethren, by the mercies of God, that you present your bodies a living sacrifice. . . . For I say, through the grace given to me, to everyone who is among you, not to think of himself more highly than he ought to think, but to think soberly, as God has dealt to each one a measure of faith.
>
> Romans 12:1, 3, NKJV

There is a tremendous amount of written material available today that addresses a person's self-image. Much of it would say that the goal of a right self-image is to feel good about yourself. The thinking behind that statement most often is that the better you feel about yourself, the more productive and fulfilled you will be.

Of course, there is a lot of truth to that statement, and you should feel good about who God has made you to be. But feeling good about yourself cannot be the final goal. What God intends in your having a right self-image is far greater than that. It involves all of the following qualities.

First, a right self-image helps you to enjoy fulfilling relationships, whether they be with God, yourself or others.

Second, a right self-image is important because it helps you to rightly reflect Jesus Christ. This is why if you are unsatisfied with the way God made you, it is extremely difficult for you to display an accurate reflection of Him. If your attitude toward God is distorted, your reflection of Him will be as well. "You are a chosen race, a royal priesthood, a holy nation, a people for God's own possession, that you may proclaim the excellencies of Him who has called you out of darkness into His marvelous light" (1 Peter 2:9).

Third, you are called to be a person who loves. In fact, the Bible commands us to love. How is it possible to fulfill this command if you hate yourself? If you do not love yourself, you will be unable to love God or love your neighbor. "For the whole law is fulfilled in one word, in the statement, 'You shall love your neighbor as yourself' " (Galatians 5:14).

Although the emphasis in this verse is on loving one's neighbor, the passage presupposes that you love yourself. Perhaps it can then be said that the way you love yourself will be the way you love your neighbor. This may account for the state of the world today—we love others about as much as we love ourselves, which is, indeed, not very much at all.

What is genuine self-love? It is not self-exaltation; it is self-acceptance and appreciation for who God has made you to be. The more you accept and love who God has made you to be, the less engrossed you become with yourself. You know who you are. It is no longer an issue.

Fourth, you are also called to be a person who serves. In John 13, Jesus provided an illustration to His disciples about serving each other. In this passage, Jesus girded Himself as a servant and proceeded to wash the disciples' feet. The task of foot-washing was particularly demeaning in that time—travelers would come in a house after having walked on dirty roads, and their feet would be sweaty and filthy. The job of washing feet was the responsibility of the lowliest servant.

> Jesus, knowing that the Father had given all things into His hands, and that He had come forth from God, and was going back to God, rose from supper, and laid aside His garments; and taking a towel, He girded Himself about. Then He poured water into the basin, and began to wash the disciples' feet, and to wipe them with the towel with which He was girded.
>
> John 13:3–5

True servanthood depends on knowing who you are. Jesus knew who He was, and so He did not regard this form of service as a threat. He had the heart of a servant and was able to serve His disciples in this way because He loved them. It was something He desired to do, not something He performed out of obligation.

Many of us can quote the verse that says if we wish to be great in the Kingdom of God, we should become the servant of all. We know that being a servant requires ultimate humility, and so we grit our teeth and force ourselves to be obedient, even though it goes completely against our nature. Even in servanthood, we can adopt a martyr's attitude, wanting others to see how much we have sacrificed in order to serve. In other words, we want others to see how great we are in our humility! Certainly this is not as much selfless as it is self-centered.

A few years ago, Bev and I decided to attend a three-month Crossroads School with Youth With A Mission in Hawaii. I have taught in other YWAM schools many times, but this time I was coming in as a student. Each student in the school was assigned work duty. My particular responsibility was helping in the kitchen every other weekend, and eventually, it turned out to be a lot of fun. Unfortunately, it did not start out that way.

As the school term began, I noticed there was something about the situation that bothered me. I realized I missed being called "Pastor Dan." I remember thinking, *I've traveled all over the world preaching. I've pastored a church for thirteen years, and all of a sudden, I'm no longer Pastor Dan! I've cleared my calendar for several months in order to attend this school, and now, here I am scrubbing pots and pans in the kitchen at the very place where I used to teach! What's going on here?*

One particular Sunday afternoon, I was begrudgingly scrubbing a pot, thinking, *They want me to serve? I'll show them. I'm going to serve them like they've never been served before!* Right about that time, one of the leaders in the school, who is also a good friend of mine, walked by. He stopped, looked at me and said, "Oh, how the mighty have fallen!"

As he walked away, I honestly wanted to take the pot I was scrubbing and bring it down on the top of his head. Of course, I did not do that. I knew he was kidding, and I probably would have said the same thing to him if the roles had been reversed. But those few words of jest touched something deep inside me. They forced me to come to terms with the fact that I was struggling with my own personal identity crisis.

I had to remind myself of what I had reminded countless people before. The fact that I was scrubbing pots and pans was incidental—my identity was not that of a pot scrubber. In fact, my identity was not that of a pastor, either. My identity was founded in the fact that I was a new creation in Jesus Christ. I was and am a son of the living God. Whether I scrub pots or am elected president of the United States, it will never have any bearing on the fact that I am God's child. That is who I am, and no job or occupation will ever change that.

When I was able to come to terms with this, I was able to accept the task at hand without struggling for position. After that, working in the kitchen became more enjoyable and relaxing. Spending my Sundays cleaning pots and pans actually became liberating, and I found myself looking forward to my time there. Our work team began doing creative things with our time, sometimes even singing for the other students at lunchtime. By the time the school had ended, I looked back on kitchen duty as one of the high points.

> Have this attitude in yourselves which was also in Christ Jesus, who, although He existed in the form of God, did not regard equality with God a thing to be grasped, but emptied Himself, taking the form of a bond-servant, and being made in the likeness of men. Being found in appearance as a man, He humbled Himself by becoming obedient to the point of death, even death on a cross. For this reason also, God highly exalted Him, and bestowed on Him the name which is above every name, so that at the name of Jesus EVERY KNEE WILL BOW, of those who are in heaven and on earth and under the earth, and that every tongue will confess that Jesus Christ is Lord, to the glory of God the Father.
>
> Philippians 2:5–11

Jesus existed in the form of God, but He did not regard equality with God as a thing to be grasped. He did not strive for it because He knew who He was. He could take the position of a servant because He knew who He was. He could become obedient even to the point of death on a cross because He knew who He was, and He was secure in His identity.

Fifth, you are also to be a person who ministers the life and power of Jesus Christ.

> When all the people were baptized, it came to pass that Jesus also was baptized; and while He prayed, the heaven was opened. And the Holy Spirit descended in bodily form like a dove upon Him, and a voice came from heaven which said, "You are My beloved Son; in You I am well pleased."
>
> Luke 3:21–22, NKJV

Just after this event, Jesus began His ministry. No miracles or ministry performed by Jesus was recorded prior to this. God states in this verse that Jesus was His beloved Son, thus establishing His identity. This identity was confirmed in Luke 4, as Jesus retreated to the wilderness and was tempted by the devil. The very first thing Satan said to Jesus was, "If you are the Son of God," which was a direct attack on His identity. Satan knew full well who Jesus was, and he sought to convince Jesus that it was not true. Indeed, if Jesus had doubted who He was for even one moment, it would have all been over.

In the same way, Satan seeks to cause us to doubt who we are in Christ. His ploy is to convince us that we are *not* a new creation in Jesus and in this way to undermine our potential. He attempts to sow seeds of doubt, bringing up questions such as, "Who do you think you are? What makes you think you can minister to others? What makes you think God deems you so special?"

In order to effectively fulfill our call to minister, we need a right sense of our identity, so that, as Jesus did, we can address the enemy directly with the confidence of knowing who we are. *You are called to be a person of triumph!*

Jesus is returning—that much is certain. However, until He does, God has a job for us to do. We are not to shut ourselves off from the rest of society to wait for His return. Instead, we are called to make a difference in the world in which we live! As the people of the Kingdom of God, we are called to extend His Kingdom to every part of the world and every area of society. We are called to be victorious, but we cannot do this if we are not secure in who we are.

You are a new creature in Jesus. And because He dwells in you and is able to accomplish anything, you can become everything God intends for you to be.

Indeed, we can be people who love. We can serve effectively. We can minister the life and power of God to those around us. And we can live triumphant lives, victorious over the pain and failure of the past!

There is hope for you!

Chapter 4

My Dog, Spot, and the Strongholds of His Life

Our first ministry assignment after my wife and I were married was a mission church located in the Highland Park section of Los Angeles. "Old Pisgah," as it was known, was not only a place where the poor and needy could find help, it also was a place of historical value. "Pisgah" was one of the key sites of the early Pentecostal revival that eventually touched much of the nation.

Bev and I had only been married about six months when Doug and Ken came to live with us. Doug was eleven years old at the time, and Ken was six. We thought they would only stay with us for a couple of weeks while their mother found a place for them all to live. We had no idea that God had another plan; but that's another story, or perhaps another book. Another thing we did not realize was that with the boys came Spot, the stray puppy they had found in a local park—it was a package deal.

Spot's name described him perfectly except for one thing: Spot was the victim of a "stronghold" that affected his ability to get along with people, especially me. Don't worry, I am not going to tell you that this little puppy was demon possessed. I would not even call it a *spiritual* stronghold. But it was a stronghold nonetheless. Spot had been deeply scarred by things that had happened to him—most likely at the hands of another man—and he believed that I was out to get him.

Shortly after the boys and Spot moved in, Spot decided to make the hallway of our house his personal toilet. Realizing what he was doing, I suggested in a rather loud voice (I guess you could say I yelled) that he should STOP! I began to walk toward him in order to restrain him from completing his business, but after I had gone only a couple of steps, the dog came unglued. I hadn't even touched him, but you would have thought I had broken his legs from the way he began to howl and cry.

I stepped toward Spot again, but before I could reach him, he ran out of the back door into a corner of the yard, where he continued to screech at the top of his lungs. By this time, I realized that this puppy was scared to death of me, but why? I had never laid a hand on him. I had welcomed him into my home with open arms, even shared my food with him. Wanting to settle the poor thing down and show him that he did not need to be afraid of me, I slowly reached out my hand to pet him while attempting to reassure him in soothing tones (isn't that what all the dog manuals say to do?) I told him, "It's all right, boy. No one is going to hurt you. There's nothing to be afraid of. I understand," and so on.

Unfortunately, Spot was so frightened that as I reached out to touch him, he bit me and then continued to howl. At that point, I should have been the one howling: I was the one who had blood streaming from my hand, not him! By this time, a small crowd had assembled. Spot and I were the center of attention.

Over the next few months, I learned a great deal about patience—and about dogs. It took time, but Spot and I eventually became good friends. He learned to trust me, understanding that I was not like the other man who apparently had abused him. I also learned something about strongholds and belief systems—how easily they can be established, how unreasonable they can become and how difficult they can be to break through.

The story of Spot provides a great illustration of some key points in understanding strongholds. Of course, it is a story about a dog. That's why I use the word *illustration* rather than *example*. Spot's situation does not describe a spiritual stronghold, just a stronghold. Spot had been conditioned by previous experiences to expect men, under certain circumstances, to abuse him. Even though I myself had never hurt him, his experience told him that I would. Spot had all the potential to become a great family dog, but his past experience filled him with fear and mistrust.

As we have already seen in previous chapters, God created us with the potential to live fulfilling and effective lives. However, the kingdom of darkness seeks to paralyze our potential and destroy our dreams. If the attempt is successful, we are left struggling with feelings of inferiority, a crippling lack of confidence and a diminished sense of personal value. Ultimately, we become unable to embrace all that God has created us to be. The devastation resulting from this demonic attack is evident in wasted gifts and unrealized aspirations.

Even our personal relationships suffer ruin from this attack. Indeed, if our self-concept is distorted, we will look to others to build our self-esteem. We can even emotionally drain those around us in our search for affirmation.

Our relationship with God can suffer as well. If we have a distorted concept of ourselves, it is also easy to distort the truth of who God is.

Tragically, without a change in our thinking, we may never accomplish the work God has ordained for us to perform as part of the Body of Christ. The forces of darkness can succeed not only in undermining our potential, but also in undermining the work God desires to perform through us in touching the lives of others. We can become so focused on trying to determine who we are that we become unable to give of ourselves, which is the basis of Christian service.

Over the years, I have discovered that much of the devastation in our self-concept is rooted in five areas that have significant influence upon our lives. These influences can result in the formation of strongholds that can lock us up and hold us captive. These five areas are:

1. Parental modeling and influence (*see chapter 5*)

2. Life experiences (*see chapter 6*)

3. Unattainable standards (*see chapter 9*)

4. Unwise comparisons (*see chapter 9*)

5. Self-talk (*see chapter 9*)

These five areas will be addressed in more detail in the following chapters, but to deal effectively with these influences, we must allow the Holy Spirit to change our mind-sets. In other words, we need to break the thinking patterns that have us convinced we can never change. "Be renewed in the spirit of your mind" (Ephesians 4:23, NKJV).

The story of the *Titanic* illustrates this point perfectly. When the *Titanic* set sail on its maiden voyage from England to the United States, officials were warned that the course they had set was unsafe. They would be sailing in waters that contained icebergs and ice flows that were extremely dangerous. They were advised to alter their course and sail farther south. Unfortunately, the officials on the *Titanic* were intent on setting a record for speed in sailing the Atlantic and the southern course would impede that record. Ultimately, they were convinced the *Titanic* was unsinkable, and so the warnings of danger went ignored.

The *Titanic* was first warned of the ice flows ahead of them on April 12, 1912, by the French liner *La Touraine*. The captain of the *Titanic* received the message and passed it on to the fourth officer, who noted that the *La Touraine* was to the north of their course.

A day later, on April 13, the liner *Rappahannock* informed the *Titanic* that they had dented their bow and twisted their rudder due to heavy ice. On April 14, the *Titanic* received a total of six separate ice warnings, the fifth one coming from the *Californian*, that indicated there were three icebergs only fifty miles away from *Titanic's* position. We don't know whether these warnings were actually delivered to the bridge, as shortly thereafter, the *Titanic* entered an area 78 miles long, filled with icebergs.

The final message from the *Californian* to the *Titanic* reflected that they were "stopped and surrounded by ice." The reply came from the *Titanic*, "Shut up, shut up, I am busy; I am working 'Cape Race.' " In response, the radio operator for the *Californian* turned his radio off and went to bed.

Just hours later, the *Titanic* struck an iceberg. Over 1,500 people lost their lives, most of them freezing to death in the cold ocean water. Ironically, the *Californian* was only a few miles away. Had their radio still been on, they would have received the *Titanic's* SOS and been able to engage in rescue efforts. It was not until flares were sent up that another passing ship, the *Carpathia*, altered their course toward the *Titanic*. By then, however, it was too late.

The officials of the *Titanic* had been convinced that nothing could sink their ship; they believed it to be invincible. Unfortunately, they believed a lie—in spite of warnings from those who knew better. They were locked into a false mind-set.

The same thing often happens to us. We may have a negative picture of ourselves that is locked into our minds. That perspective may be etched in stone, and it influences our actions, our relationships, everything about us. Even though others may compliment our good qualities, affirm us or indicate how much we have blessed them, we are convinced it is not true. We continue to believe a lie and fail to accept the truth.

Do not allow yourself to be held captive by your past. If your mind is in conflict with the Word of God, embrace the truth of His Word and break that mental stronghold.

It is interesting to note the significance of a stronghold. A *stronghold*, in the Old Testament, was a command post. It was the place where strategic intelligence was processed, and it served as a base of military operations. Often the stronghold was placed in the center of a city and secured with thick walls that were virtually impenetrable. In the event of a battle, the residents of the city would retreat into the stronghold for safety. It was a structure that effectively sealed off inhabitants from attack.

Spiritual strongholds operate in much the same way. They are constructed at the center of our belief systems, and they become the grid through which we filter everything, including our own self-concepts, our relationships with others, even our understanding of what God is like. Spiritual strongholds can be both offensive and defensive. They are protected and reinforced by the truth that surrounds them or by the lies and deception on which they are built.

While we most often speak of spiritual strongholds in a negative sense, they can also be very positive. Remember that the Old Testament picture of a stronghold is both a fortress and a refuge. David captured the stronghold of Zion and lived there (see 2 Samuel 5:7, 9). It was in that stronghold that God spoke to David, giving instructions for battle (see 2 Samuel 5:17). David wrote of God being his stronghold and refuge: "The LORD is my rock and my fortress and my deliverer; The God of my strength, in whom I will trust; My shield and the horn of my salvation, My stronghold and my refuge" (2 Samuel 22:2–3, NKJV). "The LORD also will be a stronghold for the oppressed, A stronghold in times of trouble" (Psalm 9:9). "God is my stronghold" (Psalm 59:9).

Proverbs 10:29 boldly declares: "The way of the LORD is a stronghold to the upright" (NKJV).

Second Samuel 5:7 indicates that strongholds built on lies and deception can be taken from the enemy and transformed into strongholds of truth. David took the stronghold of Zion from the Jebusites, and it became the City of David from which he ruled the nation of Israel.

> For though we walk in the flesh, we do not war according to the flesh. For the weapons of our warfare are not carnal but mighty in God for pulling down strongholds, casting down arguments and every high thing that exalts itself against the knowledge of God, bringing every thought into captivity to the obedience of Christ.
>
> 2 Corinthians 10:3–5, NKJV

Lie-based strongholds are often at the center of a distorted self-image. Remember that your self-image is the mental picture that you have of yourself. It is a picture based on conclusions you have drawn about who you are and what you are like. If your conclusions are based on lies, then your self-concept will be shaped by and reflect those lies.

I am convinced that Satan's greatest point of attack is on our understanding of who God made us to be—our identity. If he can keep us from understanding that, he can not only lock up our potential, he can also distort our concept of God, limit our relationship with Him and restrict our influence on a needy world.

Lie-based spiritual strongholds most often seek to dominate our minds and keep us from believing the truth. These strongholds can be found in families, often passed from one generation to the next. They can dominate cultures, nations and regions with unhealthy ways of thinking and even destructive behavior.

Every culture, people group or nation has its own positive characteristics, including a unique ability to express the glory of God and reflect His image. Each also has negative strongholds established by the kingdom of darkness to lock up individual potential and to distort and destroy cultural identity.

In the story of Spot, I mentioned our Native American sons, Doug and Ken. Because of them, I have become more acquainted with Native American cultures and history. I have discovered this people group to be unique—a deeply spiritual and caring people with gentle hearts and creative minds. They have an affinity with and respect for God's creation. However, the deep pain, rejection and betrayal that they have historically experienced, along with the loss of their land and personal dignity, have created a severe identity crisis. These events have also given place to the lie-based strongholds of shame, rejection, resentment, depression, broken and divided families, violence and alcoholism.

Spiritual strongholds can also be found in institutions, such as governments, universities, even churches. Ways of thinking that are etched in stone and unwilling to yield to truth can influence entire movements. For example, ministries may try to update old administrative systems or change leadership in order to achieve new success, but the spiritual strongholds that plagued them in the first place are never addressed, nor is their power ever broken. As a result, their attempts to change suffer dismal failure. The lie-based stronghold only becomes stronger and, perhaps, more deceptive.

The promise of 2 Corinthians 10:4 is that God has made available His power and the spiritual weapons necessary to penetrate the lie-based stronghold: "The weapons of our warfare are not of the flesh, but divinely powerful for the destruction of fortresses [strongholds]." Whether it is an individual stronghold, a family stronghold passed from one generation to another or a stronghold of a religious, national or cultural nature, God has given us the capacity to tear it down.

How Strongholds Are Established

Spiritual strongholds can be defined as deeply entrenched ways of thinking. They are the negative thought patterns that are so strongly etched in our minds that they govern our entire thinking processes. They become much like a grid through which all of our thoughts must pass. Strongholds are the governing ideas that we believe at a very deep level. In fact, they become part of and help form our belief systems.

Over time, these strongholds become impenetrable. They actually become the way you think or what you deeply believe. Reason, logic, the words of experts, even the truth of God's Word will find it difficult to break through these core beliefs. This is at the heart of what Paul wrote about in Ephesians 4, as he directed his readers to be renewed in the spirit of their minds:

> In reference to your former manner of life, you lay aside the old self, which is being corrupted in accordance with the lusts of deceit, and that you be renewed in the spirit of your mind, and put on the new self, which in the likeness of God has been created in righteousness and holiness of the truth.
>
> Ephesians 4:22–24

Allow me to paraphrase what I believe is being said in these verses:

"Now that you are a new creation in Christ, you have a new identity. You're not the same person that you once were. God sees you in Christ as His. To live a successful, fulfilling life, to live out all that God intends you to be, to fulfill your destiny, you've got to stop thinking about yourself the way that you have in the past. You've got to stop believing the old lies that have shaped your self-concept. They are not true. You are a new creation with a new identity. The only way you can stop believing the old lies is to allow the Holy Spirit to break through the stronghold and change your belief system (the spirit of your mind). As He does, you will start to see yourself in truth, in Jesus, righteous and holy, totally acceptable before God and equipped for every good work. But you have the responsibility to actively pursue the truth and reject the lies that you once embraced."

Spiritual strongholds are most often established in one of three ways:

1. Past experiences
Traumatic, one-time experiences or repetitive situations in our past can form the basis of a stronghold. Remember Spot? Because of his past experiences with an abusive man, he obviously believed that all men were going to hurt him. When his current situation mimicked his past, he reacted out of fear and past experience. He didn't know me. I had never laid a hand on him. But his recall of past abuse at the hands of another man reinforced the notion that I would also hurt him, and therefore, he reacted in the only defensive way he could: He bit me. Regardless of whether Spot's past experience was a one-time traumatic occurrence or a repetitive pattern of abuse, it formed the basis of his "belief system."

2. The influences of our environment
Not only have we been born into a world that is hostile to God, but we are continuously influenced by this world. Its values, standards and belief systems invade every area of our lives. The things that we read, the movies and TV programs we watch and the music we listen to all influence the way we think. The lifestyle of our neighbors, the friends we choose,

the area where we live, the schools that we have attended, the atmosphere of our homes—all of these things have an impact on our lives. Our environment is constantly seeking to conform us into its image. That is why Paul wrote, "Do not be conformed to this world, but be transformed by the renewing of your mind, that you may prove what is that good and acceptable and perfect will of God" (Romans 12:2, NKJV).

3. Willful disobedience and sin

All of us face areas of temptation, those places in our lives in which we are vulnerable and open to the attack of Satan and his kingdom. Temptation itself is not sin, but it does put us in a position of choice. Will we resist the point of attack, or will we give in to it, opening ourselves to its control? The more we repeat sinful actions, the stronger their control becomes in our lives. In time, they will become a stronghold, and we will then have little control over it.

Understanding the Nature of Spiritual Strongholds

There are three things that are important in understanding the nature of spiritual strongholds. First, *spiritual strongholds are built on the lies we believe.* Through personal experiences and our environments, including our family, culture or religious heritage, we become convinced that certain things are true, and these convictions form the basis of our belief systems. These deeply held beliefs will influence our thought patterns, emotional responses and actions.

Secondly, *spiritual strongholds are often reinforced and maintained by shame,* particularly those strongholds that affect how we see ourselves. Shame is the result of a deep sense of inferiority. It tells you that there is something deeply wrong with you that cannot be fixed. Shame declares, "You cannot change. You are hopeless."

Shame builds huge walls in order to protect our secrets, and it eventually leads to all kinds of destructive behavior, self-pity and withdrawal from meaningful relationships. Shame isolates us, or parts of our lives, and keeps us in darkness where light and truth cannot bring hope and freedom.

Third, *strongholds are consistently reinforced or defended by intimidation.* While shame makes us feel hopeless, intimidation makes us feel helpless. We cannot confront and overcome this stronghold on our own; we are insignificant and powerless before it.

After generations as slaves in Egypt, God's "chosen people" had come to believe that they were insignificant grasshoppers. Their life experience and the environment in which they lived for so long had formed a belief system, a stronghold of slavery and insignificance. They thought, felt and lived out what they believed about themselves—that they were no more significant than grasshoppers. Even though they had been led out of bondage in Egypt and they were no longer slaves in the physical sense, they were still slaves in their thinking. The reality of a slave's life in Egypt—substandard living conditions, hard labor, constant beatings, inhumane treatment and verbal abuse—all would have brought about tremendous shame and a deep sense of inferiority and hopelessness.

The children of Israel said, "Because the LORD hates us, He has brought us out of the land of Egypt to deliver us into the hand of the Amorites, to destroy us" (Deuteronomy 1:27, NKJV). After all the miracles they had witnessed and after experiencing the reassurance of God's presence—that He was for them and would fight on their behalf—they were still unable to face the obstacles before them. They were intimidated by the enemy: "We are not able to go up against the people, for they are too strong for us" (Numbers 13:31). While they remained the "people of God," which was their true identity, that generation did not break down the stronghold that kept them from living like the people of God in the land that He had promised them. Instead, they wandered around the mountain for the next forty years, believing a lie that was strengthened by shame and defended by intimidation.

Does this sound like the story of your life? If so, how is it possible to change that pattern? How can you demolish the strongholds in your life and walk in freedom?

> For though we walk in the flesh, we do not war according to the flesh. For the weapons of our warfare are not carnal but mighty in God for pulling down strongholds, casting down arguments and every high thing that exalts itself against the knowledge of God, bringing every thought into captivity to the obedience of Christ.
>
> 2 Corinthians 10:3–5, NKJV

Allow me to again share a "Sneed paraphrase" regarding the meaning of this verse in relationship to our study:

"Being a new creation in Christ and having a new identity does not keep us from normal human experiences. We face the same things that everyone else does—the same challenges, obstacles and life issues. However, we do not deal with them in the same way that others do, nor in the way that our human thinking would naturally respond. God has given us spiritual weapons that are simple and often defy human logic, but that have proven to be extremely powerful in destroying old lie-based belief systems that continue to dominate our thoughts, emotions and actions. These weapons not only destroy our old thinking patterns, but they have the ability to replace those patterns with God's truth—the kind of truth that sets you free."

One of the most powerful stories in the Old Testament is the story of a man named Gideon. His story is told in the book of Judges at the time of Israel's continuing conquest of

Palestine. Joshua did defeat strong Canaanite forces, but he did not occupy all of the land that God had given to Israel. The book of Judges describes the conquering process as gradual and lengthy.

Gideon is introduced to us in Judges 6, at one of Israel's lowest points. In a quest for success and prosperity, the Israelites had given place to the worship of Baal, the Syrian god of productivity and prosperity. As a result, they had become captives, living in caves and dens in the mountains, hiding in fear of the Midianites.

Our first introduction to Gideon shows him threshing wheat in a winepress on his father's property, hiding from the Midianites in fear and intimidation. It was in this setting that the angel of the Lord appeared to him and declared him to be a "mighty warrior" (Judges 6:12, NIV).

In reality, Gideon was anything but a mighty warrior. In fact, if I were to describe Gideon before his encounter with the angel, "mighty warrior" would be the furthest phrase from my mind. I would be more inclined to use terms such as *fearful, intimidated, confused, insecure, major inferiority complex* or even *coward*, but never *mighty warrior*. Apparently the angel saw something in Gideon that he failed to see in himself.

The angel stayed with Gideon through the process of tearing down his lie-based strongholds and replacing them with truth, in much the same way as the Holy Spirit works within our lives today. Step by step, Gideon became exactly what the angel of the Lord declared him to be—a mighty warrior.

Let me encourage you to take a few minutes and read the entire story. It is an incredible picture of how the Holy Spirit can redeem and renew our lives. And it also gives us practical insight on how to destroy spiritual strongholds.

> Now it came to pass the same night that the LORD said to him, "Take your father's young bull, the second bull of seven years

old, and tear down the altar of Baal that your father has, and cut down the wooden image that is beside it; and build an altar to the LORD your God on top of this rock in the proper arrangement, and take the second bull and offer a burnt sacrifice with the wood of the image which you shall cut down."

Judges 6:25–26

How to Demolish Spiritual Strongholds

Three actions are essential in demolishing spiritual strongholds:

1. Identify the stronghold.

When Israel turned to Baal as a source of success and prosperity, a spiritual stronghold was established. The altar of Baal was the focus of that spiritual stronghold.

Identifying the lies that have formed our belief systems and established spiritual strongholds in our minds is the first step in their destruction. The best way to identify the lie is to know the truth.

Jesus said to those Jews who had believed Him, "If you continue in My word, then you are truly disciples of Mine; and you will know the truth, and the truth will make you free" (John 8:31–32, NKJV).

After reading the story of Gideon carefully and knowing the history of Israel, I have concluded that the children of Israel believed that the key to their significance was success and prosperity. (Does that sound familiar?) Because they believed this, they were driven to seek success and prosperity. God's intention for the Israelites was always blessing. He even promised success and prosperity if they would continue to walk with Him, but that prosperity was not to be the source of their significance. The source of their significance was only to be their relationship with God.

It is important to identify the false beliefs that form your belief system as well as the strongholds that have been established in your life.

2. Confront the stronghold with truth in the power of the Holy Spirit.

"Pull down the altar of Baal which belongs to your father, and cut down the Asherah that is beside it" (see Judges 6:25). Gideon was instructed to confront the stronghold, to demolish it and to destroy the "Asherah," a female goddess that always accompanied the altar of Baal as a support. Every spiritual stronghold has its own support system, including thinking patterns, shame and intimidation.

"Do not be conformed to this world, but be transformed by the renewing of your mind, that you may prove what is that good and acceptable and perfect will of God" (Romans 12:2, NKJV). The world has a way of forcing us into its mold. The world's values, standards, priorities and attitudes, as well as its definitions of happiness and success, have had a major impact on the way we think. Probably without our even realizing it, this way of thinking has significantly shaped much of our belief systems, especially our self-image. The world has created a model of successful, valuable people—including how they look, what they wear, where they live, what kind of education they have and how they think about certain issues. This mentality says, "If I am to be a valuable member of the community, I must conform to the world's model of success." The pressure to conform is intense.

Interestingly enough, in seeking to break free from the world's mind-set, the Church has actually created a counter-culture. We address all of the same issues—from a more conservative, Christian perspective, of course—and we create as much pressure (if not more) to conform. We have defined what "good" Christians should look like, how they should act and even how they should think about certain social and political issues. If you want to fit in, then you will think, act and live out these values.

While I certainly agree that there are biblical values and standards that are very important, even essential, to uphold as a Christian lifestyle, most of us form values out of our own personal theological, political and cultural backgrounds. And in our attempt to avoid the world's mind-set, we can overreact and set standards that become idealistic, even legalistic, and have little biblical foundation.

Paul addressed this problem in his letter to the Roman Christians, warning them not to be conformed to the world (see Romans 12:2). He urged them not to allow the world, with its values, attitudes and definitions of success and happiness, to influence their way of life. In other words, they were not to allow the world to "clone" them. It would if they let it.

However, at another point, Paul also warned against "Christian cloning," or legalistic mind-sets that can become religious strongholds and rob us of genuine freedom in Christ. "It was for freedom that Christ set us free; therefore keep standing firm and do not be subject again to a yoke of slavery" (Galatians 5:1).

The world's mind-set says, "I can find purpose and significance apart from God." The religious mind-set says, "I can find purpose and significance in religious performance." Both mind-sets reflect a lie-based belief system—a stronghold that must be broken. The true source of purpose and significance can only be found when you allow the Holy Spirit to transform and renew your mind—to change the way you think.

The word the Bible uses to begin the transformation and renewal process is *repentance*. Repentance simply means "to change"—to change one's mind, purpose, actions or direction. It is a very positive word that offers a way out of the most destructive of situations.

Repentance is acknowledging the fact that you were headed in the wrong direction. Your actions and attitudes toward God were wrong and needed to change. Repentance is more than just a feeling of sorrow. While it certainly can include an emotional experience, true repentance must involve a change of mind that results in a change of actions or direction.

Repentance begins by identifying, confronting and turning from the old false beliefs that have dominated the way you think, formed belief systems and established strongholds. However, repentance is not just turning away from those things. It also must involve turning toward and embracing the truth of God's Word, allowing the Holy Spirit to renew your mind by replacing your old mind-set with truth.

3. Replace the lies with truth.

How many times I have heard John 8:32 quoted: Jesus said, "You shall know the truth, and the truth shall make you free" (NKJV). When I hear it, I picture in my mind some kind of power-encounter with truth. Truth is spoken, and immediately, freedom comes. But while I do not doubt that this can and does happen, the context of this verse presents a very different picture—one of discipleship and process. Read verse 32 again as it is preceded by verse 31: "If you abide in My word, you are My disciples indeed. And you shall know the truth, and the truth shall make you free" (NKJV).

Replacing the old lies with truth takes time. When you have believed in something deeply, it simply will not change overnight. The best way I know to break the power of old lies is to consistently apply truth. In time, the lies will give place to the truth, and new thinking patterns will be established. New thinking patterns based on truth will make you free, but strongholds will never break without the consistent application of truth.

In the appendix to this book, I have listed 69 things the Bible says about who we are in Christ. I encourage you to read through that list carefully. Memorize it. Consistently fill your mind with what God says about who you are, and then watch how the Holy Spirit will bring freedom into your life.

Chapter 5

Your Parents and You

Every summer, thousands of people in Great Britain pack their cars, vans and SUVs and head for the countryside. County fairgrounds, agricultural colleges, farms, even open fields are transformed into conference centers—literal tent cities or, as they call them, "holiday camps."

These camps are an amazing phenomenon. Some of them are very sophisticated, with all the latest creature comforts. Others are very primitive—or perhaps basic is a better word. What you bring is what you have! Rain or shine, hot or cold, the camps are always crowded, and everyone seems to love every minute spent there. Having been at dozens of those camps over the years, I have come to love them as well. They are special times full of the presence of Jesus.

It was on the last morning of one of these camps near a beautiful little town called Malvern when I experienced what I would call a "revelation day." I remember it well. It was a bright, sunny morning, a day that seemed to give birth to fresh, new understanding. I had been asked to speak to the entire camp on the subject of forgiveness within the family.

This was not a new topic for me. In fact, I had taught about this on many prior occasions, primarily to teenagers and young adults. I knew all the Scripture passages to use and the concepts to explain, and I had enough relevant anecdotes to successfully illustrate my points. I was confident that there would be a positive response.

As I finished the teaching, I sensed the Holy Spirit was touching hearts, and so I asked for those who needed to forgive their parents to stand. I could feel it in the air. Many were experiencing a significant move of God in their lives. The crowd included hundreds of teenagers and young adults, so I surmised that certainly many of them needed to forgive their parents.

As people began to stand, I found myself overwhelmed not only by the number of people standing (which rapidly became several hundred), but by the fact that most of them had gray hair! The vast majority who stood to forgive their parents were not teenagers or young adults. Many of them were in their fifties, sixties or even older. How could this be?

Immediately I began to reason that I had not been clear enough in my invitation. Perhaps they did not understand! I quickly tried to clarify, only to realize that they, in fact, had understood, and they were, indeed, responding to a real need. *What a tragedy to have lived your entire life locked up in unforgiveness, bitterness and resentment,* I thought to myself.

It turned out to be a morning of freedom and release for many, and I have never seen anything quite like it since. Young and old, teenagers and grandparents, began for the first time to forgive and let go of old hurts and pain. It was a day of revelation for many who discovered they did not have to live in a spiritual prison of old wounds. The failures and mistakes of their parents did not have to govern their lives any longer. They were free to forgive, to love again and to move on.

That day was also a day of revelation for me. I began to understand that unforgiveness, one of the most powerful forces of destruction, was not limited to age. You do not just "grow out of it." Unforgiveness must be faced, dealt with and released. This turn of events greatly intrigued me.

Shortly after I returned home, I shared my camp experience with a friend who had worked with the elderly for years. I was still deeply affected by the huge response to the message I had given that day in England. I found it difficult to understand how so many people could have lived so long under the destructive forces of unforgiveness. How much different would their lives have been if they had only received that message years before—even though I knew that this certainly could not have been the first time they had heard such a message! Why would they have waited so long to respond? How many of their life decisions had been made through the grid of bitterness? How many other lives had been wrongly influenced and poisoned through their unforgiveness—often without their even realizing it?

As we talked, my friend told me the story of an elderly great-grandmother. She was ninety years old at the time. For more than sixty of those years, she had been a highly respected and beloved pastor's wife. Her family deeply loved her. In fact, not a day went by that one of her children, grandchildren or great-grandchildren did not stop by and visit. They loved being with her. Her reputation was beyond question, and her example, until recently, had been faultless.

In recent months, however, things had begun to change. She became far more aggressive and hateful in many of the things she said, especially with regard to men. When she walked down the halls of her convalescent home and she spied a man with his back turned to her, without warning she would hit him with her cane as hard as possible. Because many of the men in this home were elderly and feeble, with legs that were not as strong as they used to be, a blow like that could send them to the floor, risking broken bones, even death.

Apparently, my friend told me, when this woman would act this way, her anger was not aimed at the men in the nursing home, but she was aiming her frustrations at her father. After each man would fall, she would let loose with a barrage of invectives. All the bitterness and hatred of a lifetime would pour out of her mouth. Her family was astonished. They had never seen this side of the mother, grandmother and great-grandmother they loved and respected. In fact, this behavior was the opposite of everything they knew about her.

The family knew very little about her relationship with her father. She rarely spoke of him, but when she did, it had always seemed to be positive. Being a pastor's wife, she knew well the Scriptures that instruct us to honor our fathers and mothers. Until this time in her life, she had carefully guarded the things she would say about her father. She carried her memories and negative feelings all very close to her heart and buried them as deeply as she could.

At ninety, however, she was becoming senile, and she was no longer in control of the things she had buried for so long, perhaps even consciously forgotten. But now all that pain began to come to the surface, often with devastating effects.

I often tell young people that they can pack their bags and move halfway around the world, but they will never get away from their moms and dads. I have come to believe that outside of our relationship with Jesus, our relationship with our parents is the most significant relationship in our lives.

It is generally accepted that much of one's life can be greatly influenced in the first five years and, in particular, by a parent's influence in that period of time. Children literally discover what kind of people they are and how they feel about themselves by how their parents react to them. Indeed, the general atmosphere in your family as you grow up contributes more to your view of yourself than any single event. Even when a child is in the womb, the mother's well-being can affect or even establish a sense of identity. Family atmosphere and parental response speak volumes to children. If the atmosphere in a family is tense, it can create tremendous insecurity in a child. But if the family atmosphere is one of encouragement and affirmation, parents can instill a strong sense of confidence in a child. Our identity can be secured or disrupted through the influence of our parents.

Such influence not only affects our self-concepts, but it also affects our concepts of God. I remember the testimony of another older lady who had been a believer for over fifty years. She had a deep love for Jesus. In fact, she equated her picture of Jesus with that of her mother, a gentle and caring woman. On the other hand, when it came to perceiving God as a loving, compassionate Father, she experienced a terrible struggle.

This woman had grown up with an abusive, alcoholic father. When she was a child, her father would return home in his horse and buggy, and all the children in her family could tell what condition he was in by the way he was whipping his horse. Simply by the sound of the whip, the children knew whether they should wait for him in the living room, hide in their bedrooms under the bed or climb out the window and hide in the nearby fields. If he had been drinking, her father would burst into the house and use the buggy-whip first on her mother and then on his children. It became clear that this woman had equated her heavenly Father with the brute that was her earthly father.

Often our concepts of God and how He relates to us is colored by our perceptions of our parents and how they related to us. As in this lady's childhood, fathers who are cruel and abusive can cause a child's concept of Father God to be the same. Some children may have had fathers who, for various reasons, paid little attention to them or perhaps were emotionally distant or not there at all. This, too, may affect their concepts of God in that they may have difficulty believing He desires to be intimately involved in their lives.

It is necessary to realize that there is no perfect father except for God. In order to overcome the deficiencies of our earthly parents, particularly our fathers, we need to discover what Father God is really like. One of the greatest needs in our world today is for the release of a father's love into the lives of his children. I am convinced that one of the most effective ways to overcome the deficiencies of our earthly parents is to find out what God the Father is like.

Dealing with Imperfect Parental Relationships

All parental relationships are imperfect. There is no such thing as a perfect parent. Only God is perfect. In my counseling with people over the years, I have dealt with many people who have been deeply scarred by wounds inflicted by their parents.

"Honor your father and your mother, that your days may be long upon the land which the LORD your God is giving you" (Exodus 20:12, NKJV). In today's world, how is it possible to instruct a woman to honor a father who molested her? How can we tell a young man to honor a father who neglected him when he was a child?

The Scriptures are explicit that if we honor our parents, it will be well with us. On the other hand, dishonoring our parents carries with it a curse. The first curse listed in the Law of Moses relates to idolatry, which is dishonoring God, and the second curse relates to dishonoring our parents. The issue of parental relationships is, therefore, an extremely important issue.

Often one of the first questions asked by a psychologist when counseling new patients has to do with their relationship with their parents. Your parents are in you. They are a part of you. You cannot get away from them. If you are unable to maintain a right relationship with your parents, it will affect every other relationship you have, including your relationships with your spouse, your children, yourself and God.

Nevertheless, it is not enough to beat someone over the head with God's commandment, saying, "Honor your parents or else!" The Word of God is meant to set us free, not threaten us. Remember the story of the grandmother in the retirement home who lashed out against the men around her? She had been a pastor's wife. She knew full well God's command regarding her parents, and she had never spoken ill of her father in her life—although it became clear that when she lashed out against the men in the home, she was actually lashing out at her father.

Jesus once said, "These people draw near to Me with their mouth, and honor Me with their lips, but their heart is far from Me" (Matthew 15:8, NKJV). It is not possible to just go through the motions of obedience. Like the grandmother, at some point, the true emotions will come to the surface. Honoring your parents is not an issue that can be effectively dealt with by rote obedience. It is a heart issue. If your heart is clear toward your parents, then you will be able to deal with them in the way God desires.

In order to effectively address issues involving your parents, particularly those areas in which you may have suffered hurt as a result of how they treated you, there are several steps you can follow that will help begin the process of healing and forgiveness.

1. Be honest with yourself, and face the areas in which your parents hurt you.

Just because you were wounded by your parents' words or actions, it was not necessarily their fault. Hurt can often be the result of how you see something or how you perceive what occurred. Even so, carefully examine how your parents treated you, honestly saying to yourself, *This is what happened, and this is how it affected me.*

2. Talk it out with a trusted pastor, leader, counselor or friend.

With a trustworthy person, discuss the areas of hurt you are facing, but do so for the purpose of getting it out of your system, to bring healing and healthy closure. If your purpose is just to criticize your parents, blame them or rationalize your own actions against them, then you will only succeed in deepening your wounds. But if you are seeking to resolve your hurt and not live under it anymore, having someone there to listen, cry with, pray and hold you accountable can help a great deal.

3. Try to put your parents in the proper perspective.

Many people believe that their parents should have been perfect, or at least better than they were. In reality, our parents are mere human beings. I have never met a parent who set out with the intention to hurt his or her child. Many of those who inflict pain upon their children either lack understanding, do not know what they are doing or act out of their own pain and suffering.

Putting your parents and their actions into proper perspective is not meant to excuse them; it is for the purpose of helping you resolve issues in your own heart, so that you are able move beyond the cycle of pain.

After speaking at a YWAM school on one occasion, I was approached by a young man who was clearly distraught. When talking with me, he shared that his parents had separated when he was a teenager, around thirteen or fourteen years old. Subsequently, he went to live with his father, a very emotionally sick man who would occasionally threaten suicide. The father would even stage his suicide attempts in such a way that his son would discover him and save him in the nick of time. The young man described instances when he would come home and find his father with a rope around his neck tied to the rafters, ready to kick the chair out from under himself, or with a gun pointed to his head with the hammer cocked. The young man would then coax his father out of the attempt.

I could see that this was a very angry young man and that these episodes with his father had affected him very deeply. When I asked if he had ever spoken to his father about what had happened, the man said he'd tried, but again it ended with his father threatening suicide. This young man had bottled up a tremendous amount of emotion with regard to all that his father did, and he desperately needed to get it out of his system. I suggested that he write a letter to his father and pour out all of his feelings. The letter would never be sent to his father—if his father were ever to read it, it might be too much for him in the fragile emotional state he was in. But I encouraged the young man to express all the anger and emotion he was feeling as if he were speaking directly to his father, and together, he and I would pray about it and talk it through.

Of course, I was placing myself into a precarious position. This young man was a football player, and offering to take the brunt of his anger might not have been one of the safest things I have ever done. But the next morning, he knocked on my door and stood there laughing nervously and telling me he had been crying all night long. I cringed a bit, thinking I had sent him into an emotional tailspin and he was cracking under the pressure.

Instead, the young man said that through the process of writing things out, he had come to the realization that his father was indeed a sick man, and yet he found he had love in his heart for his father that he never knew he had. Once he had poured out all of his emotions, he was able to see his father not just as a human being with severe psychological problems, but also as someone he cared about rather than someone who had purposely inflicted mental torment upon him.

I ran into the young man about a year and half later, and

he told me that his attitude toward his father had changed dramatically. He had a tremendous amount of love for his father and wanted to help him as much as possible. After he was able to put his relationship with his father into the proper perspective, he could deal with his anger toward his father and accept him for who he was.

4. Try to distinguish between what actually happened and your interpretation of what happened.

Usually you will find that what actually happened is not the root of your hurt—it is how you interpreted what happened or what was said that led to your emotional pain. Making this distinction is a healthy way of dealing with problems and sometimes can help you gain a new perspective on past events involving your parents.

5. Recognize that God is bigger than your parents' failures and mistakes.

God can take negative circumstances and use them to redeem your life. In particular, God can take how your parents treated you or what they said to you and turn it from something that eats at your well-being into something that can build your character. What the forces of darkness mean to destroy you, God intends to use for your good. "And we know that all things work together for good to those who love God, to those who are the called according to His purpose" (Romans 8:28, NKJV).

For example, consider the story of Joseph found in Genesis. He was a young man, thrown into a pit by his own brothers and then sold into slavery. While working in the house of an Egyptian official, he was falsely accused and then sent to prison, where he might have lived out the rest of his life. The events of Joseph's life, especially how he was unjustly treated, could have easily left him crippled by bitterness and resentment. He undoubtedly struggled with self-pity, anger and unforgiveness. But instead of becoming an emotional wreck, Joseph became a deliverer.

The account of how Joseph ascended to become second-in-command of the nation of Egypt, and how he treated his brothers later, is one of the most poignant stories in the Bible. What his brothers had intended for Joseph's destruction, God used to bring about the deliverance of their entire family. Joseph recognized that God had a greater purpose that went far beyond his unjust treatment.

6. Take responsibility for your reactions to your parents' actions.

It is important to account for your own areas of sin, confess them and repent of them, in order for the Holy Spirit to be loosed in your life and bring about the healing you need. Recognize that bitterness and resentment are sins, no matter how justified they may seem. (We will discuss this issue in more detail in succeeding chapters.)

7. Forgive your parents.

Forgiveness is a decision you make—it is not based on your emotions. I forgive others because I have been forgiven by God. I also forgive others because God has commanded me to forgive. If I refuse to forgive, then I violate Jesus, who is living in me.

Forgiveness is a process that may take some time, depending on the extent of your violation and the type of person you are. Nevertheless, forgiveness is of vital importance because it will unlock much of the bondage you live in day to day. Again, the issue of forgiveness and steps to take in order to effectively forgive will be discussed in chapter 7.

8. Choose to honor your parents.

Honoring your parents is not based on how honorably they have treated you—either as a child or as an adult. Honor is a heart issue that involves you and you alone. Honoring your parents may not change their attitudes; you must honor them even if they do not change their attitudes toward you or if they have already passed away. In some cases, your parents may not even be aware of what they have done to you.

Dealing with the failures and mistakes of your parents should not be a way of throwing their actions back into their faces. That would be nothing more than spiritual pride. These eight steps are meant to help you deal with the personal issues involving your parents that smother your ability to discover all that God intends you to be. If you can effectively address these issues, you can experience a new dimension of freedom that will positively affect every aspect of your life.

Chapter 6

Life Experiences

In an earlier chapter I gave you a very basic definition of the word *self-image*. Simply put, your self-image is how you see yourself. It is the mental picture you have of yourself, composed of conclusions you have made about your worth and value. Much of the information leading to those conclusions comes from what you have experienced in your life, especially in your childhood. Most psychologists agree that what we experience in our early years has the greatest impact on how we later see ourselves and live our lives. In fact, many believe those early experiences and our reactions to them form a pattern that we repeat throughout the rest of our lives.

The good news, however, is that you are a new creation in Christ! Jesus has the ability to break any negative cycle and replace it with truth and righteousness. Still, a new *identity* does not automatically guarantee a new *self-image*. Your old life experiences can continue to influence how you see yourself today.

When I was seven years old, I began my first church. Yes, you read that correctly. I was seven years old, and I must have been the world's youngest pastor! Every Saturday morning, I would gather all the neighborhood kids I could find into my backyard or the side yard between my house and the neighbor's. I would set up old wooden boxes, tree stumps or large rocks for church pews, and my pulpit consisted of an old orange crate. We would all sing (perhaps a stirring rendition of "She'll Be Comin' Round the Mountain"), and then I would tell my audience about Jesus. When I was seven years old, I was quite aware of God's call on my life. I was not afraid of anything. I loved people. I loved Jesus. I was a leader. All of my authority figures until that time had been positive. In school, I was not just the teacher's pet, I was the principal's pet!

This all changed, however, when I entered the third grade. My teacher that year, for some unknown reason, did not like me. I had never had a problem with authority figures before this, but this woman held something against me that, to this day, I have never understood.

On numerous occasions, she lost my homework and gave me poor grades as a result. My parents and I made absolutely sure that all my homework was completed, which I never had difficulty doing before, but it was no use. She continued to lose my work and then would say I had failed to turn it in. Furthermore, she would grade me down for it. My grades went from As and Bs to Cs and Ds. While this was frustrating, it was not beyond my ability to deal with—that is, until one memorable event that radically changed my life.

I should have gone to the bathroom five minutes before, but for some reason, I thought I could hold it. You know the feeling! Unfortunately, the pressure became excruciating, and in desperation, I stood to my feet.

"Teacher! I really have to go to the bathroom . . . NOW!" I emphasized.

She walked over to me and glared. "You learn to control your kidneys."

Unfortunately, it was not my kidneys that were causing the problem. My abdominal cramping was becoming unbearable, and I persisted in my attempt to get her permission. She still refused to give it to me. Finally, it was too late.

I could not hold it in any longer. I had diarrhea and, you guessed it, it went everywhere. I was horribly embarrassed. In my little mind, this was about as bad as it could get. To make matters worse, the kids sitting nearby immediately began to squeal and scream, "Oooh, Teacher! What smells over here?! Oooh, look at what Dan did!"

At that point, my teacher walked back over to me. Instead of recognizing the embarrassing situation I was in and attempting to alleviate things, she leaned over to me and snarled, "You dirty boy! How could you do that?!"

It was twenty minutes before recess. She made me sit in the mess the entire time, refusing to let me go get cleaned up. The derision from my classmates occasionally quieted down, but when it did, the teacher would come back over to me, hold her nose and repeat, "You dirty boy!" or "It stinks over here!" and so the class would get worked up all over again. The twenty minutes felt like twenty years. Each time the teacher spoke to me, it was like a dagger piercing my heart.

At recess, instead of going to the bathroom to clean up, I walked right past the boys' room, out the school doors and straight home. When I arrived, I told my mother of my accident, but I told her it had happened at recess, not in class. I did not want my mother to know what had really happened because, in my mind, the teacher's words, "You dirty boy," had to be the truth. I should have been able to control myself: I felt there was something wrong with me, something shameful. I also knew that if my mother became aware of what happened in class, that my teacher refused to allow me to go to the bathroom even after having had the accident, she would have gone down to the school immediately to deal with the situation, and I did not want any more embarrassment.

Something, in fact, was wrong that day—very wrong. That event served as the catalyst for the closing up of my personality. Before long, the person God had created me to be had become locked up and bound inside.

A short time after this, I was playing baseball, a sport that was quite important to my family. My father had played on a farm team for a major-league franchise in his younger days, and later, my brother was very active in Little League. On this day, I was playing in the outfield when a fly ball was hit out toward me. This was a pivotal point in the game: If I were to catch the fly ball, it would be the third out, and my team would win. But if I dropped the ball, the other team would score, and we could lose the game.

As the ball sailed toward me, high in the sky, it suddenly became lost in the sun. I tried everything to shield my eyes and catch sight of where the ball was heading, but I just could not see it. All I could do was raise my mitt and hope for the best.

I wish the story ended with me catching the game-winning fly ball and saving the day, but unfortunately, the ball hit me in the head and dropped to the ground. We lost the game.

Immediately, jeers rose up from my teammates. "You stupid idiot! You dropped the ball! How could you miss that?!"

Again, their derision cut like a knife driving deep down inside me. Their taunts weren't unusual for third-grade boys, especially when they're playing baseball, but earlier in the classroom something had happened deep inside of me, and now it was being reinforced.

From that day forward, I changed from a confident and outgoing child who was manifesting the call of God on my life to a complete and total recluse. Where I used to conduct little church services for all the neighbor kids, I now became terrified to stand in front of others. I often would skip class rather than give any type of oral report, preferring to receive a failing grade than to face the ridicule of my classmates.

It is difficult to understand the impact of certain events in our lives, the deep injuries they cause and the scars they leave. My third-grade experiences changed my life. Those words, "You dirty boy!" and, "You stupid idiot!" played out in my mind over and over again, and for some reason, I believed them.

Words are powerful tools that have the ability to shape—or destroy—lives. They can release potential, encourage vision, build confidence and bring healing. They can also steal courage and limit fulfillment. They can silence, and they can imprison. Words certainly had that effect on my life.

One of the strongest influences upon me was my grandmother. There had always been a special bond between us. I often joke that there is the Father, the Son, the Holy Spirit and Grandma—she held that kind of respect in my eyes. Furthermore, my grandmother loved me very deeply. I had no question about that.

Grandma and Grandpa had recently purchased a set of window blinds for their living-room windows. They were not the thin mini-blinds that we have today. They were the older type of wide-slatted ones popular in the 1950s. To make them work properly, you had to be very patient. If you failed to move both sides up simultaneously, you were in trouble. The more impatient you were, the bigger the problem you had opening them.

At eight years old, I was not known for great patience, and I had gotten the new blinds into one of those impossible positions: one side up and the other side down. I shook them, rattled them and twisted them, but they would not budge! In my frustration and impatience, I was literally about to pull them completely off the wall. When Grandma came into the room and saw that I was needlessly destroying her blinds, she grabbed my arm and in one unguarded moment of anxiety exclaimed, "Can't you do anything right?"

Immediately I let go of the cord, and she was able to patiently solve the problem. Words like that were uncharacteristic of my grandmother. She knew the power of her words, and she was always careful how she used them. I knew how deeply she loved me; she had always been my greatest fan. She always believed in me. In fact, in Grandma's eyes, I could do no wrong.

Realizing what she had said, Grandma immediately apologized and asked forgiveness, but those words had already penetrated my mind and locked themselves inside.

"You dirty boy!"

"You stupid idiot!"

"Can't you do anything right?"

Those words and experiences began to shape and govern the next years of my life. All the potential that God had invested in me, all of my gifts and abilities, all the dreams of a young "preacher" were bound up in what would become a massive inferiority complex.

As I entered my teen years, I was extremely withdrawn. At my high-school graduation rehearsal, I recall dreading the moment when I would have to walk on stage. It wasn't even the "real" ceremony—all I had to do was walk out, pretend to receive my diploma, shake the principal's hand and walk offstage—no verbal interaction or speeches of any kind. But the closer I got to the stage, the more nervous I became. I worked myself up into total panic, completely convinced that I would somehow make an utter fool of myself.

Even though it was just a rehearsal, I was scared to death! When my turn finally came, I drew a deep breath and forced my legs to walk out on the stage. And then disaster struck. Without warning, I vomited all over the stage and myself. Talk about a self-image builder. It was a total embarrassment!

That is how deep my fear was embedded in my heart. From the time that I was seven, I knew I was called to the ministry, and I had never forgotten that. Now that I was graduating, I knew it was time to pursue that calling, but it was the last thing that I wanted. How could I go into the ministry if I had a serious inferiority complex and was terrified of other people? How could I go into the ministry if I hated God for the way He had made me? Those questions were very real to me. As strange as it may seem, ministry possibilities were greater for me at the age of seven than at seventeen. All the potential of my young life had been successfully locked up by my life experiences.

All of us, at one time or another, deal with feelings of inferiority, insecurity or inadequacy. If kept in the right perspective, those feelings can motivate us to positive action. But for some people, they can become overwhelming, causing them to withdraw from others, build protective walls and hide from reality.

Inferiority is the deep-seated feeling that you are not adequate to face the challenges of life. It makes you feel like you are defective, incompetent or somehow not as good as other people. An inferiority complex is often rooted in one of two things: shame, which says "I am hopeless," "I cannot change" or "There is something so wrong with me that it cannot be fixed"; and second, constant or repeated failure. Failure confirms to a person with an inferiority complex that I am defective, that I cannot do things right, I cannot succeed or I am a failure. Both of these factors, shame and failure, with all of their accusations, are nothing but lies. But if we believe them long enough, they become part of our belief system, spiritual strongholds that must be broken. The inferiority complex in my life that had been birthed in both failure and shame from my third-grade experiences became a major spiritual stronghold that gave place to other points of bondage in my life.

After graduation from high school, I enrolled at LIFE Bible College. Even though I feared getting up in front of other people to preach, I was more afraid of what God would do to me if I failed to pursue my calling. In my mind, I saw God as some kind of dictator. I believed I had better do what He said—and do it immediately—or He would literally kill me. I did not understand that God was a God of love and mercy. Out of my own inner torment, I had crafted a distorted image of God. To me, He was cruel, exacting and hard. This was not an image I had been taught as a child, yet I had come to embrace this view of God without question. Therefore, my going to Bible college was non-negotiable— God had called me to ministry, and I dared not cross Him! Although my heart might not have been in it, my perception of God left me no choice.

Six months into Bible college, however, I decided I was playing a game I could not finish. I was absolutely convinced that God knew full well how petrified I was to speak in front of people, and yet He was making me go into a profession in which public speaking was a requirement. In my disturbed mind-set, God wanted to make a complete fool of me, and I hated Him for it.

For the first six months, I was pretty good at masking my feelings. No one knew how angry I was at God nor how much I did not want to go into the ministry. But one day I decided that enough was enough. I was going to quit, come what may. I recall walking straight to the dean's office to inform him of my decision.

As I entered his outer office, I asked the secretary if the dean was available to see me. She told me he was out and would not be back for another hour. *Great!* I thought. So now God was going to squeeze another hour out of my life. I left the office and went on to class to wait for him to arrive. It occurred to me, years later, that anyone else might have just left the campus and not returned. Not me. I guess I was so afraid of rejection, I was going to do things properly to the end.

In class, I somehow managed to get myself sandwiched right in the middle of a row. People to the right of me. People to the left of me. And I was so afraid of what they would think of me if I asked them to move, I was stuck!

Class began with worship. Although everything in me rebelled, I forced myself to lift my hands and paste a "spiritual" smile on my face while I joined in. Nobody could see through my façade, but inside I felt like a volcano ready to erupt. Finally it was too much. I said to myself, *I'm done with this! I'm never going to do this again.*

I dropped my hands and stopped singing. I didn't know it, but it just so happened that my actions had perfectly coincided with the end of the song. The room went silent, and I stood there with my eyes closed as tightly as possible. I knew my classmates had seen my hands go down and they must all be staring at me. Had my mask come off? Had everyone finally discovered that the guy they had thought was an angel was really a demon in disguise?

While I stood there immersed in fear, one of the students began to give a prophetic word. Somehow, I knew the message was for me, and I became even more terrified. God had gotten me stuck in this row, and now He was going to expose me in front of everyone. I wanted to crawl under my seat. I was convinced God was going to say something like, "Sneed!" (Everyone knows that when God is upset with you, He calls you by your last name.) "If you leave here today, I'm going to have a car run you down before you can cross the street!"

I stood there, like I was in third grade all over again, ready to be embarrassed and mocked by my teacher. However, when the word came, it was not what I expected. Instead, God said to me, *You can leave here today as you've planned. I will go with you, and I will bless you because I love you. Or you can stay here as I desire, and I'll set you free. I'll change your life, and I'll use you to touch the lives of many other people. But you can leave here today like you plan to, and I'll go with you and bless you because I love you.*

I was stunned. It certainly did not sound like a message from the God I knew. There was no anger or vindictiveness in the message. God had spoken directly to me, but He had done it in such a way that no one else knew the message was for me. He did not humiliate me in any way, nor did He reject me. Instead, He told me He knew exactly what was in my heart, and He still loved me. And He would continue to love me whether I did what He desired or not. For the first time since the third grade, I heard God say to me, *I love you.*

I am sure that over the years God had tried to get this message through to me, but I was not listening. I was too locked up in my own pain and inferiority complex to hear Him. But I heard Him that day—and what I heard shattered the image I had created of Him. It had been a long time since I cried, but tears welled up and streamed down my face. How could God love me that much?

I could sense the presence of God surrounding me. I quietly said to Him, "Lord, I don't even like You. And I certainly hate everything about me."

I waited for Him to fall off His throne, but nothing happened. (Do you know you can be honest with God? He is pretty secure in who He is!) And so I continued, "There's no way I can go into the ministry. I'm a basket case. I can't even talk to people. I'm so messed up. But if You really mean what You just said to me—if You really love me that much, then do whatever You want with my life."

Through my tears, the Holy Spirit broke through and touched something within me. It did not come in a dramatic "zap!" that electrified the room, causing me to jump up, grab the microphone and suddenly deliver a groundbreaking sermon. But something inside me did break, and from that moment, a process of healing ignited in my life that eventually resulted in my deliverance, restoration and miraculous emotional healing. If you had known me then as opposed to now, you would not believe you were looking at the same person. God has a done a dramatic work in my life!

I believe these events in my life are not altogether unique. We have all suffered similar events, some more horrendous than others. My message in sharing this with you is that if God can redeem my life, as bound and dysfunctional as I was, He can do the same for anyone. While Satan seeks to imprison our potential and abilities, God is ready and able to restore the quality of our lives through His healing and redemptive power.

Indeed, where God had given me the ability to speak, which was evident even when I was seven years old, through events I had experienced and words that had been spoken to me, my ability was locked up. I became deathly afraid to speak. Where I had the ability to hear the voice of the Lord and maintain a sensitivity to people, in my distorted thinking I developed a hatred of God and a fear of people that would not allow me to even carry on a conversation with those around me. But Jesus came to set the prisoners free, and that is what He did in my life. He set me free so I could develop the abilities and fulfill the purpose He had originally intended for me to realize.

All of us have gone through difficult life experiences, some more traumatic than others. Bad things do happen to good people. But not only does God have the ability to redeem those life experiences and use them for something good in our lives, He also made a promise that He will. "And we know that all things work together for good to those who love God, to those who are called according to His purpose" Romans 8:28, NKJV).

Regardless of where you have been or how deep are the emotional wounds of your past, God's power is greater. There is more power in the light of God's grace than in the darkness of man's heart. God's grace to you is always intentional, and it will overpower what any human being may have done to you, either intentionally or unintentionally.

You can walk in the transforming power of His grace, or you can continue to live in the prison of past experiences. The choice is yours.

Chapter 7

The Power of Forgiveness

Not long ago, I was watching an interview on television in which a mother and her adult daughter shared their story of forgiveness. In the past, the mother had gone into violent rages. When her daughter was young, she would fly into one of her rages and beat the daughter's head into a wall or lock her in a closet. If she got completely out of control, the mother would take her thumbs and push them into her daughter's eyes. One day, she pushed too hard, and her daughter was left permanently blind. As a result of this incident, the mother was sent to prison and denied any contact with her daughter until she turned eighteen, and her daughter was placed in a home for handicapped children.

Years later, the daughter became a Christian, and after she turned eighteen, she sought out her mother in order to forgive her. Subsequently, the mother and daughter were reconciled.

At the time the program aired, the daughter had written a book chronicling her life and the process she had gone through to forgive her mother. The mother, no longer incarcerated, traveled with her daughter to various engagements, assisting with logistics and other basic responsibilities.

Most of us would say that this daughter had every right to be bitter and resentful. When an enraged mother takes from her daughter one of life's most prized possessions, her eyesight, unforgiveness and resentment would seem only natural. But that was not what the girl chose to do. Instead of allowing unforgiveness to dominate and eventually destroy her life, she reached out to her mother with forgiveness. Because she herself had experienced the forgiveness of the Lord when she became a Christian, she explained that she, in turn, could do nothing else but forgive her mother.

We, too, can choose whether or not we remain bitter and resentful about the circumstances in our lives. You may have gone through difficult, potentially damaging experiences in your life. But no matter how significant these may have been, it is not necessary to live your life consumed with anger. We can let our past experiences eat us up inside, or we can choose to forgive, releasing those events or people to God.

One of the most remarkable stories in the Bible is that of a young man named Joseph. Joseph was the youngest son of Jacob. When he was seventeen, it was obvious that God's hand was upon him and that he was his father's favorite.

Overcome by jealousy and hatred, his brothers plotted to destroy Joseph. At first, the plan was to kill him and then tell their father that a wild beast had devoured him. Then they thought of a better idea. As a caravan of Ishmaelites passed by, they said to one another, "Come and let us sell him to the Ishmaelites and not lay our hands on him, for he is our brother, our own flesh" (Genesis 37:27).

Can you imagine the sense of betrayal and rejection that Joseph must have felt? First, his brothers had plotted to kill him, and then they sold him into slavery. As the story unfolded, the Ishmaelites, in turn, sold Joseph to Potiphar, the captain of Pharaoh's bodyguards. Over the next several years, Joseph was in and out of prison, and he experienced great favor, only to watch it turn to rejection and disappointment. Those were hard years, years that could have easily destroyed Joseph's spirit and filled him with bitterness and resentment.

As Joseph passed one test of injustice after another, he gained great favor with Pharaoh and eventually became the number-two man in the nation. This is a powerful story with huge significance. Not only is it the story of how one man, submitted to God, survived incredible adversity and injustice, eventually triumphing over it, but it is also a picture of incredible forgiveness.

Years after his brothers had thrown him in the pit and sold him into slavery, when they thought that their brother—the "dreamer"—would never be heard from again, they suddenly came face to face with Joseph. Even though his brothers were completely unaware of whom they were dealing with, Joseph was in a position of power. He had the ability to balance the scales of justice, and why not? After all the years of pain and suffering, it would have been almost too good to be true. Had God delivered his brothers into his hand to do with as he pleased? I wonder how many times, while sitting in a dark prison cell or feeling the lash of the whip as he was forced to perform a slave's task, had he, in anger, planned revenge? And suddenly the opportunity was his.

Genesis 45 contains one of the most moving stories in history. Joseph, second in command over the most powerful nation in the world at the time, lost control of his emotions and sent everyone out of his presence except his brothers. This was the moment he had decided to disclose to them who he really was.

> So there was no man with him when Joseph made himself known to his brothers. He wept so loudly that the Egyptians heard it, and the household of Pharaoh heard of it. Then Joseph said to his brothers, "I am Joseph! Is my father still alive?" But his brothers could not answer him, for they were dismayed at his presence. Then Joseph said to his brothers, "Please come closer to me." And they came closer. And he said, "I am your brother Joseph, whom you sold into Egypt.

Now do not be grieved or angry with yourselves, because you sold me here, for God sent me before you to preserve life."

Genesis 45:1–5

All the pain of a lifetime, all the locked-up emotions, the grief, the anger, the desire to get even, the need to make them pay for what they had done—Joseph released it all. The Scriptures tell us the sound of Joseph's wail could be heard throughout the palace. It was the sound of a man forgiving.

The extent of Joseph's forgiveness can be seen most clearly when he recognized the grief and fear on the faces of his brothers. Instead of delighting in their desperation or gloating in their position beneath him, he consoled them by saying, "Do not be grieved or angry with yourselves, because you sold me here" (verse 5).

I would have thought that when faced with the truth, they *should* have been angry with themselves. I would have thought that a little grief was in order. After all, they had sold their brother into slavery! They had broken their father's heart! They had lied, deceived and even plotted murder! It almost begs the question, "Joseph, what's wrong with you?! At least let them sweat for a while before you forgive them. They haven't even asked for your forgiveness yet."

But Joseph knew that God's purposes were greater than his brothers' failures. He knew long before it was ever recorded in Romans 8:28 that "God causes all things to work together for good to those who love God, to those who are called according to His purpose."

That is why forgiveness works. God is greater than our circumstances. He is bigger than those who intentionally or unintentionally do us harm. While forgiveness is not necessarily fair, it does provide a way for us to break the cycle of guilt and blame. Had Joseph insisted on fairness, had he demanded that his brothers be given what they deserved, had he allowed the pain of his life to cause him to seek revenge, the cycle of destruction would have continued indefinitely.

Forgiveness is not easy. In fact, the only thing more difficult is the alternative. Forgiveness will not automatically answer all questions or balance the scales of justice and mercy. It is, instead, an act of faith one chooses to trust God to balance those scales *in His time and in His way.* We must release into His hand the right to get even. We no longer assume the role of judge. Forgiveness means we are free.

A friend of mine by the name of Ross Tooley, who has been a leader in YWAM for years, made a statement during the Crossroads School that my wife and I attended in Hawaii. "God is obsessed with forgiveness," he said. I had never heard it put quite that way before, and it was a statement that really touched me. I believe it to be absolutely true. God is obsessed. He desires to forgive us so much that He was willing to send His Son to the cross in order to do so. He could have easily wiped out His entire creation and started all over again, but His desire to forgive, His obsession, outweighed any other possibility.

When you begin to understand the Bible's true teaching on forgiveness, you quickly realize that it has nothing to do with how you feel or what those who hurt you deserve. Instead, it is based on an understanding of five things.

1. Because I have been forgiven, I am called to forgive.

> Be kind to one another, tenderhearted, forgiving one another, even as God in Christ forgave you.
>
> Ephesians 4:32, NKJV

2. Forgiveness is a command.

> So, as those who have been chosen of God, holy and beloved, put on a heart of compassion, kindness, humility, gentleness and patience; bearing with one another, and forgiving each

other, whoever has a complaint against anyone; just as the Lord forgave you, so also should you.

Colossians 3:12–13

Since God commands us to forgive, refusing to do so is direct disobedience.

3. Jesus, the Forgiver, now lives in us.

The apostle Paul, writing to his friends at Ephesus, instructed them to "be renewed in the spirit of your mind, and put on the new self, which in the likeness of God has been created in righteousness and holiness of the truth" (Ephesians 4:23–24).

The character of Jesus is in us. The new self to which Paul was referring is Jesus living in us. He is the Master of forgiveness, and He will give us abundant grace to forgive.

4. We know the power of God to redeem.

The story of Joseph provides a perfect example of God's ability to redeem even the most difficult of situations. Joseph saw God's hand in the middle of his brothers' betrayal. He could forgive them because he knew that God would cause him to triumph in the circumstances.

But in all these things we overwhelmingly conquer through Him who loved us.

Romans 8:37

And we know that God causes all things to work together for good to those who love God, to those who are called according to His purpose.

Romans 8:28

5. Forgiveness is for us.

This may seem a little selfish, but forgiveness is one of the best things we could ever do for ourselves. I have heard it said that harboring unforgiveness and resentment is like taking poison and waiting for the other person to die. What intelligent person would do something like that? Yet that is exactly what we do when we refuse to forgive. We are the ones who suffer.

But when we forgive, we release ourselves from the debilitating effects of unforgiveness.

The Effects of Unforgiveness

1. Unforgiveness imprisons us in the past and destroys the possibility of change.

Unforgiveness not only locks us up in the past, it also often places us under the control of the person we fail to forgive. The Greek word most often used for *forgiveness* literally means "to release, to let go of, to hurl or throw away." To forgive means that I no longer seek payment for a debt owed to me, nor do I seek revenge for an offense committed against me. But not only do I free the guilty person, I free myself. It has been said that when we genuinely forgive, we set the prisoner free—and then we discover that the prisoner we set free is ourselves.

2. Unforgiveness causes self-inflicted re-injury.

The word *resentment* literally means to "feel again." Unforgiveness keeps pain locked inside where it can be felt over and over again. When Joseph disclosed his true identity to his brothers and genuinely forgave them, his cry could be heard throughout the palace. At that moment, Joseph released years of pain. He would always remember the experiences of those difficult years, as well as the rejection, betrayal and alienation from his family, but when he forgave them, the process of healing could begin.

3. Unforgiveness creates bitterness in our hearts.

Have you ever tasted something that was extremely bitter? Do you remember how your whole body reacted to it? Some tastes are so bitter that they can almost send us into shock. For a moment, everything seems to shuts down and our faces distort in reaction. Bitterness of the soul is exactly like bitterness on the tastebuds. Bitterness sends your spiritual life into shock, and it affects every other area of your life as well. It distorts your personality and can even make you turn ugly, giving you a hard face that reflects the deep wounding of your heart.

4. Unforgiveness sets the stage for further repeated conflict.
Unresolved issues have the ability to set the stage for continuous conflict. The person who refuses to forgive will often become trapped in a constant cycle of stress and anxiety. Often those who have repeated relationship problems will find that there are unresolved issues of unforgiveness in their lives.

5. Unforgiveness puts up protective walls and masks.
To protect themselves from more hurt and pain, wounded people often build walls around their hearts. But sadly, these walls will also keep out the people who do love them. Many of us become threatened when people get too close and real intimacy becomes possible. Not only do we build high protective walls, we wear masks that create a false impression of who we are and how we feel. We are often terrified that people will not like the "real us," or that we may become vulnerable to them and they will hurt us.

The Greek word *hypocrite* comes from the large mask used by a stage actor to play a part. These masks were equipped with mechanical devices to augment the force of the actor's voice. Many people today live their lives behind self-made masks, playing roles that will make them seem more acceptable, while hiding all the deep hurt and pain they feel inside.

A few years ago, I was teaching on the subject of identity to students in a creative arts school. I asked them to create a mask that, on the outside, pictured what they desired to project of themselves to others—how they wanted others to see them. But on the inside of the mask, I instructed them to create an image of how they saw themselves. I discovered that on the outside, the students generally created an image that was bright, colorful and always exciting, but the inside, however, was usually dark, distorted and sad.

I asked each of the students not only to share their masks, but to talk about it and explain what was going on inside of themselves. Repeatedly, they expressed deep hurts, disappointments, confusion and resentment. Many of them were open enough to express unresolved issues and unforgiveness that had shaped their self-concepts. Unforgiveness builds walls and causes our masks to be held tightly in place. (I will talk more about this experience with the students in chapter 9.)

6. Unforgiveness causes emotional stress.

While there are many sources of emotional stress, one of the most devastating is unforgiveness. The deep desire to "get even"—to seek revenge—can produce constant emotional unrest. Countless people live under extreme stress due to the bitterness and anger that unforgiveness causes in their hearts.

Forgiving Those Who Have Hurt Us

It is extremely important for us to forgive those who have damaged us and our self-concepts, either intentionally or unintentionally. In the testimony of my life, I shared the experience I had with my third-grade teacher who made a spectacle of me in front of the entire class. Although I do not believe that she sat down one day and decided to destroy my self-image for the next twenty years, I do believe she was intentional in what she did to me, although to this day I have no idea why. However, even though she was so cruel, almost sadistic, to me, I still had to forgive her.

The experience I related about my grandmother, on the other hand, was a different story. It would have all but killed my grandmother if she had known the damage her words caused that particular day. She had no intention whatsoever of causing me any harm at all.

Many of the emotional wounds we suffer that are of major consequence were not intentionally inflicted. Many of these wounds occurred from incidents involving those we love; generally, people are not wounded deeply by those they do not know or care for.

Parents probably account for a great deal of unintentional damage in the lives of their children, but rarely is there any real intention to cause harm. Sometimes in their attempts to make right decisions, mothers and fathers make mistakes. Unfortunately, we often misread their intentions, embellish those events and, as a result, suffer from emotional pain. Many times we blow those circumstances up to grandiose proportions; rather than examining the event under the light of truth, we prefer to believe our exaggerations.

Forgiveness is a command (see Matthew 6:9–15; 18:21–25; Luke 6:37; Ephesians 4:32; Colossians 3:13). The fact that we are commanded to forgive should give us an indication about the nature of forgiveness. In other words, forgiveness is not an emotional decision based on our feelings. Forgiveness is a choice. We must choose to forgive. And once that choice is made, our emotions will eventually follow suit.

God does not command our emotions. He commands our will and our thinking. This is not to say, however, that forgiveness will never be accompanied by certain feelings. But emotions that accompany forgiveness should be a product of the decision we make, rather than our decision to forgive being a product of how we feel.

Forgiveness is possible. But in order to accomplish it, there are a few simple steps that can help us to overcome issues that may seem insurmountable.

First of all, *it is important to forgive a person specifically.* True forgiveness cannot be summed up in a blanket statement such as, "I forgive anyone who ever caused me pain." True forgiveness deals with specific people and specific instances. For example, I had to say, "I forgive my third-grade teacher for embarrassing me in front of the class that day," or, "I forgive my grandmother for becoming angry with me when I struggled with her window blinds."

Many times, it is not necessary to confront people in order to forgive them. I never approached my grandmother about the wound that her comment had caused. I knew it would have hurt her tremendously to know what had resulted from her comment, and I am sure she had forgotten all about the incident. The problem was not her. The problem was with me. I had allowed bitterness and resentment to develop within me because of what she said, even though there was no reason to do so.

Furthermore, forgiveness is never an excuse to throw your hurt into another person's face. Even if someone has caused you tremendous harm, to go to him or her and say, "I want you to know I forgive you, but if you hadn't been such an absolute jerk, I would never have had to do this," is not what forgiveness is all about. You must deal with forgiveness in your own life. It is your problem.

The only time, I believe, when it is proper to approach someone for the purpose of forgiving him or her is when that person knows that you have harbored unforgiveness toward him or her. But when you approach such a person, all that needs to be said is that God has been dealing with you, that you forgive him or her and that you release him or her. Period. You need not add anything else. If people, in turn, approach you to apologize or acknowledge how they hurt you, be gracious and receive their apologies. But don't belabor the issue—otherwise you risk stirring the problem up all over again.

Second, *ask God to forgive the person who wronged you.*

I used to be under the mistaken impression that if I did not forgive people for how they wronged me, I was binding the hands of God from being able to wreak vengeance on my behalf. It sounds harsh, and indeed it is, but I thought that forgiveness was a way of getting even.

Forgiveness is a positive process, not only for your own restoration, but for those who have wronged you as well. On the cross, Jesus prayed for His accusers, saying, "Father, forgive them; for they do not know what they are doing" (Luke 23:34). He did not say, "Father, after You've gotten Me off of this cross, wipe these people out." Being able to ask God to forgive those who have hurt you helps turn resentment into release for everyone involved. God desires us to be instruments of healing. This is not possible, however, if you continue to hold fast to bitterness.

Third, as I have already discussed, *confess your own sins of unforgiveness, bitterness and resentment, repent and seek God's forgiveness.* This allows the Holy Spirit the freedom to begin a process of healing and restoration in your life.

Fourth, *ask God to release the emotions that have stored up inside you.* The longer you have harbored unforgiveness, the more the emotional reservoir within you has filled. The way you think about the person who wronged you, and the opinions you have formed about what happened, continually play upon your emotions. Whenever you think of that person or consider the events that happened, your emotional reservoir continues to fill. Eventually, the dam will burst.

It is interesting to note, however, that when God begins to empty out our stored emotions regarding unforgiveness, He does not break the dam all at once. Much like a literal dam, if our emotional reservoirs have too much water in them, it isn't smart to throw a stick of dynamite in there and just blow it up. The resulting flood would devastate everything in its wake! Instead, dam workers open the floodgates slowly, allow some of the water out and then close the gates. There is a period in which the gates are opened and closed in stages, until the dam is sufficiently emptied. God performs the same process in us. Our emotional makeup is not necessarily constructed to handle abrupt changes, and so a longer process is required to release our stored-up emotions little by little.

Fifth, *ask God to heal your memory regarding how you were wronged.* Although God is certainly capable of wiping away your memory of that instance, generally that is a rare occurrence. When I refer to God "healing your memory," I am referring to His touch of healing upon the continuing sting you experience from what happened to you. God can and will free you in areas where the pain of that memory has locked you up.

I can still recall in vivid terms what happened to me on that particular day in the third grade when my teacher embarrassed me. But today that memory does not bother me in the least. God has set me free from all of that. The sting of my memory and the debilitation that resulted are gone, even though I still recall what happened.

Human beings are very complex creatures. When memories are too painful or gut-wrenching, we have a natural mechanism that kicks in and shifts that memory into our subconscious. The memory is not stored up front, and so we aren't required to face it immediately. But even though it may be filed somewhere back in the recesses of your mind, that painful memory can still have a tremendous effect on your life.

You may be someone who is experiencing these types of emotional difficulties. You may know that something is wrong, yet you cannot seem to put a finger on what the problem is. In such a situation, it is important to pray and ask God to bring whatever is affecting you to the forefront of your mind. If there is something in your past that needs to be addressed, trust the Holy Spirit to bring it to your attention.

When I was a pastor, a lady in our congregation approached me one day and said, "Dan, I don't know what's wrong with me. My husband and I have been married for eight years. I love him so much, but I can't stand it when he touches me." This couple had three children, but she explained that having an intimate relationship with her husband was very difficult.

Her parents were separated, and she had a good relationship with her father, although she did not trust her mother. She had a brother whom she absolutely detested, even though she did not know why. "He tries to build a relationship with me," she said, "and even though I'm a Christian and he's not, I just can't stand him."

We prayed and talked some more. It became clear that if the situation did not resolve soon, her marriage would be over. I surmised there was something buried deep in her subconscious that needed to be dealt with, and so that was the direction of my prayer for her. At that time, however, nothing came up.

Weeks passed. One Saturday morning, I arrived at my office and found her sitting in the foyer, sobbing uncontrollably. As I brought her into my office, I did my best to try to calm her down. "What's wrong?" I asked.

"This morning, my husband rolled over in bed and put his arm around me. I went cold, like I always do," she said, "but then a picture flashed in my mind, and I screamed and jumped out of bed. In my mind, I saw a picture of my brother raping me when I was younger. Suddenly all of these memories flooded back into my mind. After the rape, I remember telling my mother about it, but she blamed me and refused to allow me to tell my father. Even after it happened two or three more times, she refused to do anything about it."

The Holy Spirit had brought out the memory of what her brother had done to her all those years before. Sometimes, after suffering traumatic events, we block such memories out. This memory explained a lot of things: why she could not trust her mother, why she had so much hatred for her brother and why she did not want her husband to touch her. That morning, however, the Lord moved upon her and began to set her free. She was able to understand and express the pain she held deep inside her. She was also able to help her husband understand the emotions she was struggling with. When he learned what had happened to her, it broke his heart. Subsequently, they grew closer together.

In addition, this woman was finally able to deal effectively with her feelings toward her mother and brother, although this was not something that occurred overnight. It was a long process, but it all began with the Holy Spirit bringing forth a traumatic experience that had been repressed for years.

While this was the way God chose to heal this woman, there may be some things you are not required to remember, and if that is the case, it is better to leave it alone. If there is a need for a memory to come out in order to be effectively dealt with, the Holy Spirit will do this without your having to dig it up. Much has come to light recently about false repressed memories being brought out in therapy. It is true that memories can be repressed, but it is important to carefully work through the process of unlocking them with a trusted counselor.

After forgiving someone who wronged you, you must consistently manage the way you think about that person. Often when we begin to work through the process of forgiveness, we may confess, we may repent, we may go through all the steps of forgiveness discussed here, and we receive a measure of emotional release. But two or three days later, that person may cross our minds again, and all the memories of what he or she did play out like a movie in our minds. Soon we find ourselves chewing up the situation all over again, dredging up all of those negative emotions, and before long, we may feel as if we have not forgiven the person at all. We may feel guilty, thinking to ourselves, *Something must be wrong with me. I just can't forgive that person. God must not forgive me, either.* Indeed, it can be terribly frustrating.

If you have experienced these feelings and believe that the process of forgiveness does not work for you, please understand that your problem is not with the process. For as long as you have harbored unforgiveness toward the person who wronged you, your mind has maintained negative thoughts about that person. These will not disappear overnight. Furthermore, because your mind governs your emotions, your emotions regarding that person will not disappear overnight, either. Therefore, you must begin to deal with the way you think about that person.

Resolve that whenever negative thoughts about that person arise, you will immediately say to yourself, *No. I forgave him or her.* Sometimes it helps to write down the good qualities of that person or the good things he or she has done for you in order to remind yourself. If necessary, whenever negative thoughts arise, pull out that piece of paper and dwell upon the positive things you have listed. In other words, focus on what that person has done right, not on what he or she has done wrong.

Usually the people toward whom we harbor bitterness are those we love the most. But we can so cram our minds full of negative memories that we forget the good things they have done for us. The key is to begin emptying your mind of those negative thoughts and replace them with positive ones. In the rare event that this person has actually done nothing good for you, then think about the good things that Jesus has done for you or the good things He could work in that person's life.

For some people, reading the Bible helps them get their minds off such negative thoughts. I have found that for myself, I need to get up and find someone to talk to and force my mind off the situation. Whatever your situation, it is important to get tough with yourself; otherwise you run the risk of falling back into the same pattern of bitterness and resentment. Forgiveness does work, but it requires effort on our parts to change the way we think about the situation or the people involved.

The final step of forgiveness is to *ask God to bless the person who wronged you.* This can be the most difficult step, as it involves seeking the benefit of those who have not done so for you. But if you have worked through the previous steps in this process of forgiveness, it is a fitting resolution. Not only will God bless that person, but you will find your life blessed as well.

One of the best pieces of advice I have ever gotten was to "keep short accounts." In other words, if someone has wronged you or something negative has happened to you, do not dwell upon it. *Deal with the issue immediately.* Bitterness and resentment can destroy both your life and the lives of those around you. This is why the issue of forgiveness is so central to the heart of God, and as such, it should be at the center of our lives as well.

Chapter 8

Leaving Your Past Behind

> Not that I have already obtained it or have already become perfect, but I press on so that I may lay hold of that for which also I was laid hold of by Christ Jesus. Brethren, I do not regard myself as having laid hold of it yet; but one thing I do: forgetting what lies behind and reaching forward to what lies ahead, I press on toward the goal for the prize of the upward call of God in Christ Jesus.
>
> Philippians 3:12–14

A Sneed family treasure hangs on our front porch—a double swing that my grandfather bought shortly after the end of World War II. I can remember as a young boy sitting with Grandma and Grandpa on that swing for what seemed to be endless hours, listening as they told stories that helped shape my life.

My grandparents grew up in the farm country of south-central Iowa and moved to Los Angeles in the early 1920s. My grandmother's stories almost always revolved around the spiritual awakening that was taking place in L.A. during those days. She would often tell us of the incredible things she witnessed in the early days of Angelus Temple, which seemed to be at the center of that revival. She recalled the miraculous healings that emptied stretchers, wheelchairs and body braces. She recalled seeing thousands of people come to Jesus, their lives transformed by the touch of God's

Spirit. She would tell stories with such detail and passion that I always felt like I was there when it happened.

It was on that swing, listening to my grandmother's stories, that I first discovered what Jesus was really like and was introduced to the power of the Holy Spirit.

My grandfather's stories, however, seemed to center around his boyhood, spent on the family farm near Centerville, Iowa. He would tell us about the cold north wind that blew across the barren Iowa hills in the winter, or the warm summer days he spent playing in a nearby river. He, too, was a great storyteller.

Several years later when I first visited the hills of southern Iowa, I found it to be just as he described. While I never remember him calling his childhood the "good old days," that is certainly what he meant. Over the years, I came to realize that there was a part of my grandfather that had never really left the farm. There seemed to be times in his life he did not want to acknowledge were over. Although in his adulthood he had achieved a great degree of success and had, among other things, become the best grandfather you could ever want, a part of him remained unable to leave the past. I later discovered that his adolescent and young-adult years had been full of heartbreak, family tragedy, betrayal and struggle. I think Grandpa preferred to dwell on the happy times of his life rather than on the painful times.

Rather than reliving happier days, however, many of us continue to relive the sins, failures and suffering we experienced in the past—all of which continue to keep us locked up and unsuccessful. Try as we may, we just cannot seem to get beyond the past.

Bitterness and resentment are among the biggest problems in the Body of Christ today. Remember, the word *resentment* means "to feel again." It is like a cancer that continues to recur, causing you to feel the painful wounds of your past over and over again. Left "untreated," that pain will affect every area of your life and, tragically, even impact the lives of those whom you love.

Second Kings 5 relates the story of Naaman and a young Jewish slave girl. Naaman was the commander of the Syrian army and was responsible for conducting raids against opposing nations (Israel being one of them), at which he had been greatly successful. Naaman was an honored and well-respected commander, but he suffered from leprosy, a debilitating disease in which parts of the body die and fall off, beginning with the extremities.

During one of Naaman's raids against Israel, he took captive a young girl who was probably about eight to ten years old. More than likely, either she had been forcibly taken from her family, or her family had been murdered by the Syrian soldiers under Naaman's command. In either case, this young girl had probably suffered significant trauma in the separation from her family. These days, psychologists would agree that suffering such a severe trauma at that young age could have scarred her for life with, quite possibly, little hope of recovery.

The Bible says that after this young girl was captured, she became a servant in Naaman's household, waiting upon his wife. I wonder what I might have done if I were in this girl's position, captured, taken from my home and forced to serve the very person who had taken me captive in the first place. I doubt I would have looked upon Naaman with much compassion. In fact, if I discovered he was a leper, I might have even rejoiced, knowing that he was going to die a long, horrible death. How good of God to allow me to watch it! Naaman had destroyed my life, and now he was going to suffer. But that was not this young girl's attitude. Upon discovering Naaman was suffering from leprosy, "She said to her mistress, 'If only my master were with the prophet who is in Samaria! For he would heal him of his leprosy' " (2 Kings 5:3, NKJV).

Instead of relishing the opportunity to see the person who had caused her such pain literally eaten away before her eyes, she informed Naaman's wife of a prophet (Elisha) who would be able to heal him.

I have never been bitter or resentful without good reason. In fact, it is easy to justify holding a grudge against someone who wronged me. Certainly of all people, this young girl would have been justified in bitterly resenting Naaman. But she didn't. As a result, Naaman went to the prophet and was healed.

It is interesting to me that the Bible does not say anything about the trauma this young Jewish girl would have experienced. By the time she informed Naaman of Elisha, it is clear she had put her past behind her and was seeking to bless those who had wronged her. What an incredible testimony to the power of forgiveness!

Here is an important point that I don't want you to miss: After you have dealt with your unforgiveness, bitterness and resentment, let them go and move on. Remember, the word *resentment* means "to feel again," and, of course, "to feel again" means "to hurt again" or "to be angry again." Do not go back there. It's over. Move on toward all that God has for your future.

The story of Naaman and the servant girl also illustrates another aspect of leaving the past behind. Once Naaman had been informed of the prophet who had the ability to heal him, he immediately traveled to the prophet's house. Naaman expected Elisha to welcome him with all the pomp and formality due someone of his stature. But as he pulled up to Elisha's house, there was no red carpet. In fact, Elisha sent out a lowly messenger to greet Naaman and instruct him what to do in order to receive his healing—wash himself seven times in the muddy Jordan River! Naaman had expected Elisha to meet him as he stood in his chariot, expected that Elisha would wave his hand and cause

Naaman's leprosy to magically disappear. What actually occurred was not what he had expected at all, and he became furious.

> His servants came near and spoke to him, and said, "My father, if the prophet had told you to do something great, would you not have done it? How much more then, when he says to you, 'Wash, and be clean'?"
>
> 2 Kings 5:13, NKJV

Naaman subsequently overcame his anger, went down to the Jordan as Elisha instructed and was healed of his leprosy. Had he continued to hold on to his expectations, angered that he was not treated the way he thought he should have been, Naaman would not have experienced his restoration.

Leaving the past behind involves leaving behind all of your failed expectations, as well as your hurt and pain. Perhaps God did not do what you wanted Him to do. Maybe there were others in your life who failed to meet your expectations, and you were deeply disappointed as a result. Failed expectations can rob you of the hope you so desperately need to successfully move through life. The writer of Proverbs declared that "hope deferred makes the heart sick" (Proverbs 13:12, NKJV).

Naaman was angry because his expectations were not fulfilled. He was certain he knew how his healing should take place, and when it did not happen that way, his hope was gone. The result was a sick, angry man.

The world is full of sick, angry, bitter people whom Jesus desperately wants to heal and set free. That same proverb goes on to state, "But when the desire comes, it is a tree of life."

Naaman's angry response to his unfulfilled expectation caused him to turn away from his only hope. Had it not been for his servant, who brought him face to face with the reality that obeying the word of Elisha was his only possibility of healing—he had nowhere else to go—Naaman would have died a bitter, angry, sick man.

While leprosy is not as prevalent in most of the world today as it was in Naaman's time, unfulfilled expectations still rob people of God's best. All of us have experienced this type of disappointment. Remember, however, the Holy Spirit has the ability to turn our disappointments into "His appointments." That's what Naaman experienced when he let go of his unfulfilled expectations and obeyed the word of the prophet. The Scripture says, "His flesh was restored like the flesh of a little child, and he was clean" (2 Kings 5:14, NKJV).

In another instance in the Old Testament, God challenged a new generation of Israelites to go in and possess the Promised Land, after Moses had died: "Moses My servant is dead. Now therefore, arise, go over this Jordan, you and all this people, to the land which I am giving to them—the children of Israel" (Joshua 1:2, NKJV).

At first, this might seem like a strange way to begin one of the most significant stories in the Bible. But God was saying, "The past is over. If you want to move on, let it go! Moses is dead. It's time for you to arise! Move on to all that I've promised you!" That message is as true for us today as it was in the days of Joshua.

One of the greatest challenges many of us face is dealing with the issues of our past. Nothing stifles our ability to successfully inhabit all that God has promised us more than living in the failure, mistakes and suffering of the past. If we are unable to effectively deal with them today, they will come back to haunt us in the future, often with devastating results.

In reality, the minute we receive Jesus as our Savior, we are accepted by God. Our sins are forgiven. However, the effects and consequences of the negative experiences in our past may continue to plague us. There is no way to hide that. We cannot simply put a bandage on the wounds of the past and hope that they will magically go away. They must be dealt with before we can effectively become all that God desires us to be.

> Not that I have already attained, or am already perfected; but I press on, that I may lay hold of that for which Christ Jesus has also laid hold of me. Brethren, I do not count myself to have apprehended; but one thing I do, forgetting those things which are behind and reaching forward to those things which are ahead, I press toward the goal for the prize of the upward call of God in Christ Jesus.
>
> Philippians 3:12–14, NKJV

God fervently desires you to be free from your past so that you can be released to pursue your future. That release can be found by yielding to the following steps.

1. Understand the grounds of your acceptance by God.

God's love is unconditional, but His acceptance is conditional. There is only one indisputable condition for His acceptance, and that is the blood of Jesus.

> For it was the Father's good pleasure for all the fullness to dwell in Him, and through Him to reconcile all things to Himself, having made peace through the blood of His cross; through Him, I say, whether things on earth or things in heaven. And although you were formerly alienated and hostile in mind, engaged in evil deeds, yet He has now reconciled you in His fleshly body through death, in order to present you before Him holy and blameless and beyond reproach.
>
> Colossians 1:19–22

2. Face and deal with the unresolved issues of the past.

Seeing yourself from God's perspective can be a tremendous help in forgetting your past. As I have stressed, you are a new creature in Christ. God sees your past sins and failures as forgiven and forgotten (see 1 John 1:9). As far as God is concerned, they have been completely dealt with.

In light of His forgiveness, it is also important to deal head-on with painful issues stemming from negative experiences that continue to plague us. As we are able to understand our acceptance by God, we can face those unresolved issues without fear of rejection, knowing that in Christ, we have been made new.

3. Allow the grace of Jesus to move into your situation and bring healing.

The only way to successfully resolve the issues of your past is to allow the grace of Jesus to touch those difficult areas of your life. The story of Gideon is an excellent illustration of this principle. "The Angel of the LORD appeared to him [Gideon], and said to him, 'The LORD is with you, you mighty man of valor!' " (Judges 6:12, NKJV).

During that period of time, the nation of Israel was suffering from constant raids by the Midianites, nomads who would sweep into the country and plunder it of any resources they could find. The raids were of such ferocity that the Israelites would literally run for the hills and hide in caves because they were so afraid. It had been that way for years.

When the Angel approached Gideon, he was busy beating out wheat in a winepress. The significance of Gideon's using a winepress to beat out the wheat is that winepresses were usually located in low, sheltered areas where workers would stomp out grapes, filtering the juice into huge vats. Wheat, on the other hand, would usually be beaten out on a threshing floor, located in wide-open areas where the wheat kernels could be thrown into the wind and separated from the chaff. Beating out wheat in a winepress was just not done, because there would have been no wind to winnow it. Gideon had probably been reduced to winnowing wheat by actually blowing on it himself!

Gideon was forced to resort to this excruciating exercise in survival primarily because, like the rest of his country-men, he was terrified of the Midianites. He and all the Israelites were bound in fear, too frightened to act as though they were the people chosen by God. Rather than risk his life on a threshing floor, Gideon chose to beat out wheat down in the shelter of a winepress.

It is into this situation that the Angel of the Lord appeared before Gideon and declared him to be a "mighty man of valor." Gideon must have thought, *Hey, Angel of the Lord, did you forget your glasses? Anyone with any amount of intelligence can see that I'm a coward! All of us Israelites are cowards because we're hiding in the hills instead of fighting for the land that God gave us.*

However, the Angel of the Lord affirmed Gideon and declared him to be something that, in the natural, he was not. This is exactly how God responds to all of us. Once we are in Christ, we are accepted by the Father. He declares us to be His children. He declares us to be righteous. He declares us to be mighty men and women of God. But He does not stop there.

The Angel remained with Gideon and walked him out of his past, a past marked by fear and cowardice. Eventually Gideon did, indeed, become a mighty warrior. He engaged in battle and succeeded, leading Israel to victory over the Midianites.

God has declared us to be new creatures in Christ. He then works to walk us out of all the pain of our past, so that we can live out all that He has declared us to be.

Many years ago, a huge piece of marble was delivered to a workshop located in a cathedral in Florence, Italy. This piece of marble had been brought from the quarries of North Africa and was deemed extremely choice—with one exception. Somehow, during the process of extraction from the quarry, a huge gash appeared right down the middle of it.

Upon its delivery in Florence, sculptors from all over Europe were summoned to examine the marble and determine if it could be salvaged. Each of them examined the marble and remarked on how beautiful a piece it was; but they all agreed that because of the gash, it was completely worthless. Nothing could be done with it.

Time passed, and the stone continued to sit in the workshop. No one touched it. Finally, it was decided that a contest would be organized to find someone who would be willing to sculpt this piece of marble. The sculpture of whoever was able to do so would be displayed at the front of the cathedral for all to see. Of course, every sculptor who has ever lived would have given anything to have his or her art displayed in such a fashion—and so, again, the sculptors examined the stone to see if something could be done.

One young man, in particular, had been asking about this piece of marble ever since it had been delivered. But because of his age and inexperience, he was continually put off in the hopes that one of the "greats" would rise to the challenge. Unfortunately, even with the contest in mind, none of the great sculptors could determine a way to salvage the piece of marble. Ultimately, the young man was given his chance and allowed to work on it.

The man worked day in and day out, twelve to fourteen hours a day over a period of months, shaping and carving the stone until his sculpture was finally completed. On the day that it was to be unveiled, people from all around the region gathered to behold the result. The tarp was removed and there it was—Michelangelo's *David*!

In the hands of a master sculptor, even a damaged piece of stone can become a masterpiece. In fact, the statue of David was the first sculpture of its kind to display movement in form. Because of the gash, Michelangelo was forced to swirl David's hips in such a way that the gash could be removed. As a result, he paved the way for an entirely new form of artistic expression. Michelangelo had a vision for what could be done with that piece of marble, even though all the great sculptors of the day had considered it worthless.

In the same way, God has a vision for your life, regardless of the mistakes you have made, the dumb things you have done or how imperfect your upbringing may have been. God has put His Holy Spirit within you to work out all of those areas of your life that otherwise could be considered a detriment. Indeed, in the hands of the Master, you can become a masterpiece!

> Beloved, now we are children of God; and it has not yet been revealed what we shall be, but we know that when He is revealed, we shall be like Him, for we shall see Him as He is.
>
> 1 John 3:2, NKJV

4. Forgive!

We have addressed this issue at length in the preceding chapter. Nevertheless, the issue of forgiveness is of such prime importance, I cannot reiterate it enough. Forgive!

5. After having dealt with the issues of your past, forget about it and get moving.

> Brethren, I do not count myself to have apprehended; but one thing I do, forgetting those things which are behind and reaching forward to those things which are ahead, I press toward the goal for the prize of the upward call of God in Christ Jesus.
>
> Philippians 3:13–14, NKJV

Remember the story of the young Jewish girl in Naaman's household? Her ability to put the past behind her and help bring about the healing of Naaman, her master, not only testifies of the power of forgiveness, but is an excellent example of God's ability to restore and transform. "So Naaman said [to Elisha], ' . . . Your servant will no longer offer either burnt offering or sacrifice to other gods, but to the Lord' " (2 Kings 5:17, NKJV). Because that young girl was able to resolve the issues of her past and move on, she was able to provide the means whereby Naaman could resolve the issues of his past and move on.

Everywhere I go, I meet people from every age group who are locked in the past. Some of them are still living in the "glory days," past triumphs and achievements—the "good old days." But for the most part, I meet people who live in the failures and mistakes of yesterday. Sometimes those failures are their own; sometimes they are the mistakes of others around them. The one thing both of these have in common is the ability to lock you up when Jesus came to set you free!

Many of us are so trapped in the issues of yesterday that all of our emotional resources are being spent on them. When we desperately need to move forward, the past has locked us in.

One of the secrets of Paul's success can be found in his words "forgetting what lies behind and reaching forward to what lies ahead." Paul recognized that the prize that awaited him far outweighed the struggles of his past. He was a new creation in Christ, and he could not live in yesterday any longer.

That discovery set Paul free and set the course for his future. That same discovery has the power to set us free today and lead us to our destiny.

Chapter 9

The Mask Maker's Game

For as he thinks within himself, so he is.

Proverbs 23:7

As class began, I was not sure what to expect from this group of creative arts students. I had asked them just the day before to undertake an unusual project. I now wondered how it would all turn out.

We had been discussing the subject of identity, self-image and the "masks" we often wear to protect ourselves—to project an image we want others to see, rather than what we really feel about ourselves. In order for them to gain understanding, not only of the subject but also of themselves, I asked them to paint a picture. The picture was to be of a two-sided mask. One side of the mask was to depict how they wanted people to see them; the other was to depict how they actually saw themselves. The plan was for them to present their masks to the class with a brief explanation of why they had painted them the way they did.

I hoped my students would be open and honest in this exercise because I knew it could open a door for ministry and healing where needed. However, since we had only been together for a couple of days, I was not sure if they were comfortable enough with me yet to be that transparent.

After a short time of worship, the students began to share. One by one, they showed the masks they had painted and gave a brief explanation of what the mask represented, both how the students wished to be seen and how they actually viewed themselves.

It was an extremely emotional morning. The students opened their hearts and, in many cases, shared their deepest pain. My heart ached for them as they revealed their work. As the class continued, however, I began to notice several things that were common to each presentation. The detail and creativity of their work was astounding. Each mask reflected their unique personalities. But regardless of background, personality, gender or age, each student wished to be seen as acceptable, capable, successful, valuable and happy. The message was always the same: "I want to be loved and accepted, and I'll do whatever is necessary to make that happen."

While in most cases, the outside of the mask (how they wanted others to see them) was bright, colorful, exciting and creative—some even quite elaborate—the inside of their masks (how they actually saw themselves) was, in direct contrast, plain, dark and even a little sad, usually constructed with much less creativity.

As the students shared about the inside of their masks, two things became apparent. First, there was a significant difference between how they saw themselves and how they wanted to be seen. It was also clear that most of their attention and creativity was focused on creating the right image to successfully mask their insecurity and brokenness. As I listened to the students open their hearts and honestly share how they felt about themselves (some for the first time), I became aware that in their search for significance and desperate need for acceptance, they, like all of us, had created masks to cover the insecurities and inadequacies of their lives.

The real tragedy, however, was that those same masks had kept them from discovering all that God intended them to be. So much time and stress was spent projecting the image of what they desired others to see, but their real need was for a revelation of the heart of God for them. They had been "masking" the lie-based strongholds that had dominated and devastated their lives, when Jesus had given them power to demolish them.

In chapter 4, we defined *spiritual strongholds* as "deeply entrenched ways of thinking"—negative thought patterns that become the foundation of our belief systems. They become the grid through which all other thoughts must pass. Simply put, a spiritual stronghold is a place in our lives or thinking processes that is dominated by false beliefs and used by the kingdom of darkness for destructive purposes.

Jesus could have easily been describing the purpose and function of spiritual strongholds when He said to His disciples, "The thief comes only to steal and kill and destroy" (John 10:10). Spiritual strongholds, like the thief himself, steal our understanding of truth, our sense of value and our identity. They kill our potential, as well as destroy our ability to become all that our Creator intended us to be. Strongholds destroy the hope of ever realizing our destiny and fulfilling our dreams.

On the other hand, Jesus said that His mission was to bring abundant life: "I came that they may have life, and have it abundantly" (John 10:10).

> ▶ **Jesus came to demolish the strongholds that the kingdom of darkness has established in our lives, releasing us to become all that the Father intended us to be from the beginning.**

We have previously discussed two areas in which lie-based strongholds are often established: parental relationships and life experiences. There are, however, other areas in which strongholds can affect how we see ourselves. In this chapter we will examine three of the most significant of these areas.

The Lies Behind the Mask

There were several important lessons I learned that day in class as the students explained why they designed and painted their masks the way they had. However, the most important lesson was rather unexpected. As each student shared, I began to realize that the *mask itself* actually explained the *student.*

The way the mask was designed and painted, as well as the image it projected, said a great deal about the students' values, what they believed was important and what they would look like and do if they felt they were significant people. The masks they had created revealed deeply entrenched beliefs that, in many cases, had become strongholds.

All of us have deeply held beliefs that have developed over the years. The primary source of these beliefs is our life experience—the influence of our parents and families as well as the educational, social and spiritual environments in which we have grown up. These beliefs, whether true or false, strongly influence every aspect of our lives, including our self-concepts, our sense of emotional well-being, our happiness and how we interpret and respond to current situations.

Identifying these deeply held beliefs, or foundational lies (as I often call them), is the first step toward freedom. "You will know the truth, and the truth will make you free" (John 8:32).

To walk in freedom, you must change the way you think. You do that by confronting and replacing the lies with truth and then guarding that truth carefully. This is such an important point that I want to make it again. The process for confronting these "foundational lies" is:

1. **Identify the false belief.**

2. **Confront the lie with the truth of God's Word.**

3. **Replace the lie with the truth.**

4. **Guard the truth.**

I call these false beliefs "foundational lies" for two reasons. First, they often become part of the foundation of our lives, part of our belief systems, and we then build our lives on them. Second, they are the foundation on which other lies are built. Simply defined, lies are beliefs or expectations that don't fit reality. Foundational lies include deeply held beliefs such as, "To be successful, I must never fail"; "Happiness depends on circumstances and possessions"; "It's easier to avoid my problems than to face them" and "It's not my fault, so I don't need to take responsibility."

For most of us, our initial response to these statements is: "I don't believe that!" People don't really think that they can succeed at everything they do. Neither do they think that they will be loved and accepted by everyone. But deep inside, many of us struggle with a profound, entrenched belief that we must never fail and that we must have the love and approval of everyone around us.

In both the developed and the developing nations of the world, success is all but worshiped, and failure has become the unforgivable sin. For many, failure can be fatal. We are driven by success, which most often is defined in terms of perfection.

Please do not misunderstand me. I'm not making a case for mediocrity or laziness. Striving for excellence is important. Developing your gifts and abilities to the fullest, using them with skill and understanding and investing them in the success of others is a significant key to personal fulfillment. But your value as a person and your acceptance before God has absolutely nothing to do with how successful you have been in reaching your goals or how much you have personally achieved.

Setting unreasonable, unattainable standards and fearing failure will only cripple and destroy you. Most perfectionists know at some level that being perfect is impossible, but lowering their expectations to a reasonable level is nothing short of admitting defeat and is a direct assault on their self-esteem. They must meet certain standards to feel good about themselves. To accept anything less than what they see as perfection is unacceptable.

The fear of failure can become a destructive enemy, producing anger, resentment, depression, lack of motivation, anxiety and even chemical dependency. But failure can become our friend if we choose to learn from it, grow through it and never allow it to define who we are.

One of the things I most appreciate about the Bible is how honestly it reveals the failure of its heroes. They were real people, facing real situations, sometimes with great success and other times with great failure. Look at the lives of Abraham, Moses, David, Peter and other great heroes of the faith. They committed acts of murder, adultery, selfishness and fear. Yet those failures did not sum up the extent of their lives. God redeemed their failures and strengthened their faith in the process. Their failures did not become their legacy—their faith did.

If it were ever possible to become the perfect pastor, I believe I did my best to accomplish that. As I began my first pastorate, I knew that to be the perfect pastor, I would have to be an inspiring preacher, a powerful worship leader, an insightful counselor and a shrewd administrator. I would be on a first-name basis with everyone in my congregation from infants to seniors. I needed to be "cool" with the teenagers, be intellectual with the college crowd and provide family fun for all the young families in my church.

I was convinced that a perfect pastor was as much at home

drinking tea with the older ladies as he would be talking sports with the young men in the congregation. I should be able to fix the church vehicles, repair the plumbing and electrical problems for the sanctuary, be adept at accounting, effectively organize special events and be productive at fundraising. Most of all, the perfect pastor needed to be the perfect husband, father and all-around role model.

As you can imagine, it wasn't long before I realized I was in trouble. Being the perfect pastor wasn't easy, especially for me. If I had tried to repair a vehicle, chances are it would cost more to fix my so-called "repairs" than if I had just taken it to a mechanic in the first place. The same went for my plumbing and electrical work. My attempts at accounting caused more than one CPA to pull their hair out over my "creative" financing. In fact, many of these responsibilities are simply not my thing, and I would do well to let others handle them. But as a young pastor in my first church, I thought that my success depended on doing all of them well.

What I found was that I had set a standard of perfection that went far beyond my call and ability, and certainly beyond God's expectations. I had convinced myself that in order for people to see that I had what it took to be a successful pastor, I had to fulfill that standard of perfection. I had a deeply entrenched belief that to be valuable and worthwhile, I had to be successful. I could not fail, and I had to have the acceptance and approval of everyone around me.

Where did my false belief come from? While it may have been passed on through numerous messengers, it originated in the brokenness of our humanity, separated from the source of our acceptance and value. It also came from the father of lies who continues to work his destruction in human personalities, feeding us lies that keep us from understanding God's intended purpose for us and living in the acceptance and fulfillment provided by the work of His Son on the cross.

These foundational lies can become so strong and so intricately woven into the fabric of our lives that we often fail to recognize them, and yet they form the foundation for much of our belief systems, thinking processes and decision-making.

In chapter 4, I introduced you to Spot, the dog with the strongholds. Spot was the stray dog that Doug and Ken found just before they came to live with us. Bev and I had just been married six months when our world changed overnight. An eleven-year-old, a six-year-old and a stray puppy suddenly became part of our family. What was intended to be a temporary situation, perhaps for a couple of weeks until their mother found a place for them all to live, turned into the rest of their growing-up years. We were not much more than kids ourselves, and against the advice of almost everyone, we took on the responsibility of raising two young boys, the oldest quickly approaching his adolescent years.

My relationship with Doug and Ken taught me more about the Father-heart of God than I ever imagined possible. I learned of the depth of His love, the length of His patience and much more than I ever wanted to learn about the extent of His heartbreak. Doug and Ken also taught me, and continue to teach me, a great deal about myself and some of the foundational lies against which I still guard.

In fact, as recently as the writing of this chapter, I came face to face with the foundational lie that had prompted my response to a situation that had taken place more than fifteen years ago. Doug had done extremely well during his teenage years living with us. He had maintained a high grade point average in school and had become a champion swimmer, ranking first place in the city of Los Angeles with his butterfly stroke. His coach had believed that with the right training and continued hard work, Doug could have become an Olympic swimmer. He had aspirations of going to the U.S. Air Force Academy and eventually becoming a commercial pilot. But some of the choices that he made in his late teens sent him in a different direction—choices that were based on foundational lies that he believed and strongholds that had not been demolished. Doug's next few years were marked by his running from God, drug addiction and tremendous heartache.

While speaking at a summer camp in England, I received a phone call that informed me that Doug had been arrested and was facing criminal charges. The call came as I was about to leave my hotel room and go to the camp, where I was to be the evening speaker. There was no time to process what I had just been told. There was no time to feel the pain or to let it out. I simply had to go.

As I drove to the camp, still in shock, the Holy Spirit whispered to me, *I want you to talk about "rebellion" tonight. There are a number of kids in trouble here and a lot of hurting parents. Tell them your story.*

My immediate response came strong and quick: *No! I won't! You can't expect me to! If I go anywhere near the subject of rebellion, I'll break down, and it won't be pretty! No one wants to watch a grown man cry!*

Several more times before the service began, the Holy Spirit would whisper to me, *Talk about "rebellion."*

Each time I would decline: *I can't do it. I won't do it! Get someone else! I would be more than happy to give up some of my speaking time!*

That night, the camp leadership had arranged for several groups to do skits depicting camp life, and of course, there were those that poked fun at the speakers (including me). It was great! I laughed so much, and emotionally, it was just what I needed. Just as they finished, the Holy Spirit whispered again, *Rebellion.* This time I felt like I could do it. The laughter had been a great emotional release, so I thought, *All right. I can handle this.*

I spoke from 1 Samuel 15 about King Saul and his rebellion against God's directive to destroy the Amalekites. He refused to take responsibility for his sin when faced with it, seeking to blame others for his sin instead. Then I told the camp what had happened to me that day and a little about the events in Doug's life that had led him to that point. Then I did exactly what I did not want to do: I broke down and began to cry.

That night, God visited the camp in a very powerful way. Teenagers and young adults filled the aisles. Parents soon joined them. It was an incredible night of repentance, release and healing. The tape from that evening became a best seller and has been used to touch huge numbers of hurting parents and broken teens. The Holy Spirit always knows what to do.

It was just the other day that I had another encounter with the same Holy Spirit who had whispered in my ear that evening, *I want you to talk about rebellion tonight.* This time, His message was a little more pointed, and perhaps even a little surprising. This time He pointed out the foundational lies that I had believed and that had shaped much of my response that night at camp.

I had always believed that my motivation for not wanting to share Doug's story that night came from a desire to protect him from embarrassment and the judgment of others, and while I do believe that was part of my concern, the reality was that I was protecting myself. I didn't want to be seen as a failure. Deep inside, I believed that I should have been able to change him. If I had been a good father, then he would not have been in that situation. And not only had I failed as a father, but also as a spiritual leader. Spiritual leaders do not have these kinds of problems with their children, regardless of their age and the circumstances.

Do you see the lie? It went even deeper than that. I believed that if I failed, I would lose the love and acceptance of those whom I respected and needed to respect me. The fear of failure is a strong motivator, especially if it is linked (and it almost always is) to acceptance and approval.

Behind every mask is a lie. Perhaps many. If it weren't for these lies that have become so much a part of our thinking, there would be no need for our masks. Remember, the first step to freedom is to identify the foundational lies that govern much of our thinking and motivate our actions. Trying to change our behavior without identifying its source, confronting it and replacing it with truth will only create the need for new masks. Jesus came to expose lies to the truth, to break their power and demolish strongholds—not simply introduce a behavior-modification program. That would never work.

Remember these four words:

- Identify
- Confront
- Replace
- Guard

The more lies we believe, the more unhappy and emotionally troubled we become. In reality, most of our unhappiness is not caused by our circumstances, but by the lies that we believe, the root cause of most of our emotional struggles.

The War Behind the Mask

Healthy competition can create an atmosphere of excitement and fun. It also encourages us to strive for excellence and become more than we ever thought we could be. Competition can be a great building tool if it is healthy and kept in a balanced perspective.

Over the years, each of our kids has been involved in some type of competitive sport. Bev and I have sat on the sidelines, watching and cheering, laughing and crying, through endless games and competitions.

I have seen firsthand the value of competition. It pushes you to develop your abilities, to give more than you thought you had. It also teaches you discipline and focus. But while competition has its healthy side that encourages growth and development, if misused, competition can become debilitating and destructive. Tragically, many of us compete for value and significance. The positions we hold, the possessions we obtain, our physical appearance, talents, abilities, social standing and even our spiritual gifts can become part of a competitive drive to "be someone."

The advertising moguls of Madison Avenue have capitalized on this competitive drive for the purpose of selling their products. They market an image that dictates to us, "Successful, valuable people wear these types of clothes," or "drive these types of cars," or "eat at these types of restaurants" or "drink these beverages." Their message, though completely deceptive, comes through loud and clear: Purchasing their products will make you valuable. They will give you a sense of confidence and bring fulfillment to your life. The advertising executives create a successful image, and we buy it!

Tragically, we in the Church have created yet another level of competitive issues and cloaked it with spiritual terminology. For many, spiritual experiences have become a point of status, as if we were competing for position in our standing before God. Spiritual gifts, ministry results, even points of self-denial and personal sacrifice are used to measure one believer against another. While I strongly believe in the development and use of spiritual gifts (they are needed today more than ever), and I acknowledge that ministry results are important, neither of these were intended to determine value, nor is self-denial or personal sacrifice a barometer of spiritual significance.

The apostle Paul, writing to a young church that had experienced the unique touch of God yet was plagued by excess, jealousy and competition, warned: "For we dare not class ourselves or compare ourselves with those who commend themselves. But they, measuring themselves by themselves, and comparing themselves among themselves, are not wise" (2 Corinthians 10:12, NKJV). Bluntly, Paul was saying that Christians who compare themselves or their ministries with other people or ministries, or who measure their success against another person's or ministry's success, just do not get it! They lack understanding and are not wise!

The obvious question follows: What do they lack understanding about? The answer is, they lack understanding of the results of comparing and measuring themselves against other people. Such behavior can have devastating consequences. *It can lead to a paralyzing sense of inadequacy, a sense of unfairness, growing resentment, a spirit of competition and a failure to be and appreciate who they are.*

Let's examine these results for a moment.

There are two types of inadequacy. One is healthy, bringing us to the realization that we desperately need Jesus. This inadequacy is the knowledge that we cannot accomplish our salvation without Him: "Not that we are sufficient of ourselves to think of anything as being from ourselves, but our sufficiency is from God, who also made us sufficient as ministers of the new covenant" (2 Corinthians 3:5–6, NKJV).

There is also an unhealthy, *paralyzing sense of inadequacy* that leads to despair and hopelessness. This inadequacy focuses our attention on our inabilities and magnifies our inadequacies to the point where we cannot move forward in faith and confidence.

This leads to *a sense of unfairness* and one of Satan's most successful points of attack. This point of attack is so successful, in fact, that Satan used it when he approached Eve in the Garden. God had instructed Adam and Eve, "You are free to eat from any tree in the Garden, but you must not eat from the tree of the knowledge of good and evil, for when you eat of it, you will surely die" (see Genesis 2:16–17).

But Satan twisted God's words and asked Eve, "Indeed, has God said, 'You shall not eat from *any tree* of the garden'?" (Genesis 3:1, emphasis mine)—a question that completely distorted what God had actually said to them. Eve responded by repeating God's instruction, but adding that that if they *touched* the tree of the knowledge of good and evil, they would die—another distortion (see Genesis 3:3).

Satan's implication to Eve was that God was being unfair: "God doesn't want your eyes to be opened. He doesn't want you to know the difference between good and evil. He doesn't want you to be like Him. God is limiting your development and possibilities. He is so unfair." And Eve bought it, hook, line and sinker.

A sense of unfairness will always lead to *resentment.* If you feel that God is unfair, you will begin to resent Him, and it's impossible to have a right relationship with someone you resent. I wonder if this isn't at the root of a lot of spiritual problems. Because we see God as having been unfair, we resent Him, and our relationship with Him suffers. It is hard to trust His love when you see Him as unfair.

It can be very difficult, especially for Christians, to deal with feelings of resentment toward God. We're not "supposed" to have those feelings, but many do. Left unresolved, resentment can be a destructive force in our lives.

Recently I spoke with a once-successful missionary who had sacrificed everything to follow Jesus, but who was allowing unresolved resentment to control his life. He could not understand why God required sacrifices of him that He didn't seem to require of others. In fact, others who had sacrificed much less, seemed to prosper more. Why?

Believe me, I've asked this question more than once. Although I don't have a complete answer, I do know that we can trust the character of God. He is always just and fair. His love for us is always complete. I also know that situations are different, just as people are different and require God's individual dealing.

A confused, perhaps even bewildered Peter struggled with this question when his breakfast appointment with the risen Jesus turned into a deep, personal encounter. Why should he have been surprised? Divine appointments are almost always like that. After they had finished eating breakfast, Jesus asked Peter a piercing question that went straight to the heart: "Simon . . . do you love Me more than these?" (John 21:15). Twice more, Jesus asked the same question, as if to probe His disciple's heart even more. Peter must have wondered why Jesus was repeating Himself. "You know all things; You know that I love You!" Peter replied to Him (John 21:17).

It might have been that Jesus was giving Peter the opportunity to "undo" the three times he had denied Jesus (see John 18:15–27). Nevertheless, Peter was probably a bit unsettled by Jesus's persistence.

At this point, Jesus described to Peter some aspects of his future—including his death. Peter, perhaps stunned by this prediction, turned to see another disciple, John, who had always seemed so close to Jesus, and Peter asked the question, "Lord, and what about this man?" (John 21:21).

This was a question that many since have asked when faced with the stress and difficulties of life: Why me? Why not someone else? Even though the response from Jesus may seem somewhat abrupt (perhaps unloving), it addressed the heart of the issue: "What is that to you? You follow Me!" (John 21:22).

Unwise comparisons will always open the door to the possibility of resentment. Even though I may be able to justify my bitter feelings with the skill of a prosecuting attorney, resentment will always build walls and restrict the flow of genuine love. If gone unchecked, it can also deal a deathblow to meaningful relationships.

While I may not understand why God allows certain things to happen and I do not understand why He deals differently with people, I do know that because I am His child, He will always do what's best for me. He has information and insight that goes beyond what I could ever know. On those grounds, I choose to trust Him. Genuine questions are never sinful. God is, without a doubt, big enough (and secure enough) to handle them. But some questions do not have easy answers. When faced with difficult circumstances, it is important for you to choose to trust Him, even if you don't understand His reasons.

Earlier I related the story about Doug. When he and his brother, Ken, came to live with us, they became part of our family in every way. Our hearts immediately knit together with theirs. When Doug became a young adult, his life began to go in a different direction. For several years, rebellion seemed to rule his life. I could write a book on all that I learned during those years, especially about the love and grace of God, as well as His power to sustain. Eventually Doug began to get his life back together. He married, had a daughter and seemed to be on the way to recovery. Then the unthinkable happened. Doug was murdered.

Any death is difficult to deal with (especially the death of a young person), but murder carries with it a tremendous sense of violation. I remember the thoughts that raced through my mind when I was informed of Doug's death.

Why? How could this happen? Where was God when Doug needed Him? What about the promises of God?

I had already struggled with many of those feelings throughout the years of Doug's drug addiction. He had used hallucinogenic drugs that had horrible mind-altering effects. I worked as the director of Teen Challenge in Los Angeles (a Christian drug rehabilitation program) and could tell story after story of young men we prayed for whom God had touched, delivered, healed and miraculously restored their minds. Although Doug had come a long way in his recovery, there were still serious scars. I recall struggling with the fact that God had healed so many of those young men for whom I had prayed, but not Doug. It was difficult to understand why this was so.

I was teaching in Switzerland when I received the awful telephone call that informed me Doug had been murdered. On the long flight home back to California, questions flooded my mind. As I sat on the plane, I said to the Lord, *Okay, I've got a list of things You promised me concerning Doug. We've got twelve hours on this plane, and I need answers. It's no longer a matter of understanding the situation.* Everything I believe *hinges on this. I cannot go on in the ministry if You don't give me any answers.*

As the flight progressed, the Lord answered each of my questions. I would say, *This was the promise. It didn't happen.* Then the Lord would show me how the promise had been fulfilled. It was not fulfilled in the way I had imagined, but it had been fulfilled nonetheless. I discovered that I had been strong-arming God, intent on making Him fulfill His promises to me about Doug in *my* way, not in *His* way. But on that flight home, the Lord graciously revealed to me how He had fulfilled His promises to me to the point where all I could say was, *Yes. I see it now.*

When I got to the final promise on my list, however, there was no understanding. I very clearly recall God's promise to me that Doug would stand beside me in ministry. But it hadn't happened. I remember saying to God, *Here's the big one. There's no way out of this. This promise was not fulfilled. Doug never stood with me in ministry. What happened?*

For the next several days, there was no answer. And I really didn't see how God could come up with one. It just hadn't happened—that seemed all too clear. Toward the end of Doug's funeral service, a friend of mine, Chuck Girard, was singing a song he had written, entitled "Name Above All Names." As I listened, it was as though the Lord began to speak directly to me. In my mind, I looked back to the day I had spoken to the camp on the subject of rebellion and told them a little of Doug's story, the choices he made and the heartache those choices had brought. I remembered the response from hundreds of teenagers and their parents that night, as well as the transformed lives that followed. I remembered the tape from that evening and how it affected so many; the letters that had been sent telling me how Jesus changed their lives and called them to ministry because of that night and Doug's story. As Chuck sang, it became so clear: *All those years Doug did his own thing, and we had little control over that. But now, there's nothing more the enemy can do to him, and we have control over his testimony and over sharing the message of what Jesus had done in his life and in ours.*

I realized that God was saying, *Do you see? Doug does stand with you in ministry.*

It was not in the way I would have wanted God's promise to be fulfilled. And even though I had my answer, I still struggled with the idea that it seemed so unfair. God could have worked a miracle, just as He did in the lives of so many others I've prayed for. Why didn't He do it with Doug?

God had not done things in the way I wanted them to be done. I had to accept that. Then, I needed to choose to trust Him. I had to lay down my own ideas about what I thought should have happened and recognize that my perspective is extremely limited. God knows all things. He sees all things, and He does have my best interest at heart.

Since Doug's death, I have had the opportunity to speak with many people who have experienced tragic events in their lives. In those conversations, I have discovered that resentment is a big issue in the lives of many Christians. Not only do we compare what God has done with what we think He should have done, we also try to compare how God works in our lives with what He does in someone else's. Over and over, I have seen that resentment can choke out everything that God desires to do in us and for us.

When we compare ourselves with other people, *a spirit of competition* often develops. Our motivation becomes, "I've got to be as good as you are, and I'll do whatever it takes. If I have to max out my credit cards to buy the latest clothes in order to look as good as you, I'll do it! If I have enough money saved to buy a Ford, but instead decide to go into debt to buy a BMW so I can appear to be valuable, I'll go into debt! I will starve myself and do whatever I need to in order to reach a certain size, so that others will accept me and love me." At that point, something's deeply wrong.

There is nothing wrong with wearing the latest clothes or driving the best cars. And we certainly want to be the best we can be. But if your motivation is, "Anything you can do, I can do better," or, "I've got to do this in order to be loved and accepted," then you're being driven by a spirit of competition.

A spirit of competition is not the same as striving for excellence or doing the best job possible. It's competing for love, acceptance and approval, and it destroys. This same spirit permeates much of the Church. Too often, church leadership promotes a spirit of competition with the congregation down the street. Somehow the ministries run by our church must be better than those of any other church in town. But the results of this competition bring nothing but hurt and frustration. Our self-image must be based on accepting ourselves as we are, and not on competing to be the best, or better than others.

I want to become all I can be. I want to develop my gifting and abilities for the purpose of investing in others—giving of myself to those around me, not competing to be better than others so that I can feel valuable and important.

When we become obsessed with comparing ourselves to those around us, we fail to become who God has made us to be. If we are trying to be like someone else, we are doomed to failure. We cannot and will not be anyone other than ourselves. It's ironic that we spend so much time trying to be like other people when it's impossible for us to be exactly like them.

On the other hand, you are guaranteed success at being you! Nobody else in the world can be you. There is no competition involved in being yourself. You are guaranteed success at being the best *you* there could ever be. You are a unique creation—a gift of God. But if you fail to be who God has made you to be and instead get caught up in trying to be like someone else, you will not only frustrate yourself trying to do the impossible, you will also rob the Body of Christ of the gift of who you are.

There is nothing wrong with admiring the qualities of another person and desiring to emulate those qualities, working his or her character into your life. But if you become consumed with thoughts of obtaining his or her gifts or reputation simply so you can find love and acceptance or gain status and position, you will never find fulfillment. There is a big difference between recognizing the qualities of a person's life—and seeking to work them into your own—and trying to become that person in order to obtain acceptance.

It is possible to be so wrapped up trying to be someone you aren't that you rob yourself of the joy of being who God made you to be—unable to enjoy the gifts He has given you.

Discover the gifts God has put within you and develop them to the fullest. Then, use them for God's glory.

The Voice behind the Mask

In the early years of our marriage, Bev often found it helpful to write me notes about feelings she was struggling with in her life. Writing often helped her process those feelings. She would give those notes to me to read during the day, and then we would discuss the situation together that evening and work through her feelings.

On one particular occasion, Bev wrote me a note relative to a situation she was working through (unrelated to our relationship), put the note into an envelope and placed it on the dresser in our bedroom. On the envelope, she jokingly typed, "Pastor Dan."

Unbeknownst to her, one of the elders in our church who wrote small devotional articles for the church bulletin, Manuel, had called me to say he had written a new article that he wanted me to read. I told him I would not be able to get to it for at least a week, but I suggested he drop it by my home or the church office at his convenience and I would eventually read it.

Later that day, I discovered the envelope on my dresser addressed to "Pastor Dan." I assumed it was the article from Manuel, so I promptly put it into my briefcase and went to the office.

The next evening I noticed there was something eating at Bev. It seemed as if she was upset, and so I asked her what was wrong.

"Nothing," came her terse reply. Of course, every husband knows that when your wife answers, "Nothing," it really means, "Something."

I probed a little deeper, but she refused to indicate why she was so upset. I decided that the best thing I could do for the moment was to back off and give her some space. Perhaps it was something she was still trying to put together in her mind, and we would discuss it when she was ready.

The next day, however, she seemed even more upset. Again I asked, "What's wrong?"

This time she replied, "You know exactly what's wrong." She said nothing more. I looked at her, completely mystified. I had no idea what she was talking about.

Later that day, I took her out to lunch hoping we could get to the bottom of this. As we sat at our table, I told her, "Look, I honestly have no idea what the problem is. I'm concerned that it's something very important and you think I know, but I'm really dumbfounded."

"What really hurt me," she divulged, "is that you took my letter and completely ignored it, as if you don't care about what I'm going through."

"What letter?" I asked.

"The letter I wrote to you," she indicated. "I left it on your dresser. You had to have seen it and taken it."

"I don't have a letter from you," I replied.

But Bev would not let up. She told me she put it on the dresser in an envelope with my name on it, and then it was gone. She had looked all around to see if it had fallen on the floor. It had not. She had also checked with the kids to see if one of them had taken it. They had not. Therefore, she concluded that I must have taken the letter.

"I don't have a letter from you," I maintained.

"You have to have it," came her angry response as she glared at me, "and what really hurts is that I poured out my feelings to you, and you didn't even bother to respond. I guess you're so busy with everyone else's needs and problems, you don't have time for me anymore."

That stung. I did not even begin to know how to respond. Our conversation ended unresolved. She was convinced I had her letter. I knew I did not.

Later that afternoon, Manuel came into my office and handed me an envelope.

"What's this?" I asked.

"It's the article I wrote for you to read," he said.

"But I got that a couple days ago," came my reply.

We stared at each other for a moment, then it hit me. Like a sack of cement falling on my head, it hit me. I reached into my briefcase with a sense of dread and pulled out the envelope I had found on the dresser. Quickly, I ripped it open, and there it was, the letter Bev had written to me. I left my office immediately and made a bee-line for home in order to profusely apologize to my wife.

What had enflamed the situation for Bev was not the facts about what occurred, but the "spin" she had put on those facts. In her mind, even though I maintained I did not get her letter, it was gone. She had checked around and could find no other explanation as to why it was gone, so therefore, in her mind, I must have taken it and been completely indifferent to her situation, caring for others more than I cared about her. She arrived at her conclusion in a precise and logical manner, but she was completely unaware of my conversation with Manuel. Unfortunately, she reached the wrong conclusion.

Even though her conclusion flew in the face of all she knew to be true about me, in particular how I always responded to her notes in the past, she still chose to believe the worst. How many times have I myself done exactly the same thing? We all have!

Allow me to make a strong statement that may rattle some of you spiritual giants out there: While you may think that the most important conversations you have are with God, I'm convinced that the most important conversations you have are those you have with yourself. These can have an even greater impact on your life. Before you react, let me explain what I mean.

No matter who you talk to, whatever discussion you carry on with another person or with God, you then immediately begin to talk to yourself about those conversations. You make decisions based on conclusions derived from your inner discussion, or "self-talk."

When we have conversations with God, or anyone else for that matter, we have another completely different conversation running simultaneously in our head. It is that of our inner voice, which is interpreting, redefining, accepting or rejecting what is being said to us.

Many times we make incorrect conclusions about our circumstances or conversations that lead to rationalization, misunderstanding, even disobedience. Your perception of what happens or what is said becomes more important to you than what actually occurred. Our "self-talk" makes all the difference in our lives and tells us what kind of people we are.

We must never underestimate the power of self-talk in our lives. It has been said that talking to yourself is normal—but when you begin to answer back, it's time for therapy. The truth is, however, we do this all the time. And these are the conversations that we believe, most of the time without question or challenge. Unfortunately, many of us have talked ourselves into a lot of hurt, pain and misunderstanding.

Looking back on my own life, I know this to be the case. Most of the deep emotional hurt I endured came from things I told myself. My third-grade teacher may have spoken harsh, demeaning words that wounded me, but the damage she did was minor compared to the damage done by the things I told myself about what had happened. I took the incident in the classroom and my teacher's ridicule, exaggerated and twisted them in my mind and ended up with an extremely distorted self-image.

I'll never forget the day I stepped out of the elevator on the fourth floor of LIFE Bible College. It was only a few weeks after the life-changing encounter with Jesus that I told you about in chapter 6. I was determined to break out of my shell and begin to build new relationships. Standing in the small lobby area just outside the classroom was a group of five or six of my classmates.

Everything in me said, "This is it! Go for it! Join the group! Get to know them!" But at the same time, my mind, still conditioned for rejection, said to me, "You're crazy! They don't want to talk to you! They think you're a nerd!"

However, I was determined. This was my chance. I headed straight for them, mustering all the courage I could, when suddenly they broke up and headed their separate ways! I was stunned.

Immediately, my mind, with all of its negative self-talk, began to say, "I told you so! They saw you coming, and they didn't want to talk to you! They don't like you, you misfit!"

I went from courageous to cowardly in a matter of seconds. I never thought that, perhaps, they did not even see me coming. And, if they had, why would they think I was coming to talk to them? I never had done so before. So what I said to myself in those few seconds could not logically have been true!

There are ways of overcoming the traps set by our "self-talk." First of all, *clearly look at what happened—just the facts*. For example, in my wife's case, she could have said, "I wrote a letter to my husband, and he did not respond." Or I might have said: "My teacher called me a dirty boy when I was eight years old." In other words, determine the basic facts about the events that occurred in your life, without making any kind of interpretation about them.

When something hurts us, we immediately want to project our opinions into the middle of it. Instead, differentiate between what actually happened and what you are projecting onto what happened. Stick to the concrete facts.

Then, *examine what you are saying to yourself about the situation*. Distinguish between the basic facts and how you evaluate those facts.

Having established the concrete facts as best you can, ask yourself, *What am I trying to say to myself about this situation?* For example, "My husband did not respond, therefore I must not be important to him." Or, "My teacher called me a dirty boy when I was eight years old, therefore she must be right, and there must be something wrong with me." Too often, we accept our self-talk as the final word on the matter. But where do the facts end and feelings and emotions begin?

Feelings and emotions are important. God created them as a window to reveal what is going on inside of us. Of course, this does not mean our emotions are always right, because what goes on inside of us isn't always right. But recognizing the role emotions play in our lives can give us a better perspective on how to evaluate them. It is never healthy to ignore your feelings and emotions, but it is also not healthy to allow your feelings and emotions to dictate how you respond to every situation.

Next, *challenge your conclusions*. Get tough with yourself. What grounds do you have to draw such conclusions? Is it possible there are other explanations for what occurred? For example, could someone else have taken the letter? Could the letter have been misplaced? Or, could the teacher have been going through some personal problems? Perhaps she had some personal grudge against me due to something that happened to her in the past.

Challenging our conclusions takes discipline. It is not always easy to do since our self-talk is the loudest when our emotions are inflamed by what we perceive someone has done to us. This is significant because the conclusions we draw may be completely wrong, and responding from wrong conclusions will only exacerbate the situation. Too many people have fallen into this trap. Reactions based on wrong conclusions can result in your making major life decisions that will have serious impact on your future. I have done this in my life, and I have seen countless others do it. The consequences I endured for doing this have been painful and emotionally damaging. In retrospect, I wish I had challenged the conclusions I had drawn rather than accept my distorted feelings as fact.

In order to challenge the conclusions that arise from personal interactions, it may be helpful to ask the other person involved some questions about the incident. But in doing so, it is important not to make threats or accusations. Loving confrontation can be a powerful force in resolving conflicts, but doing so does not come naturally. Most of us would rather close up and walk away than confront someone, especially if the conflict was heated. But how many relationships have been destroyed because someone walked away thinking something about the other person that was not true?

Of course, there is always risk involved in confronting someone we love. It is not comfortable to do so and may lead to rejection. Nevertheless, such confrontation can lead to positive results. When someone says something hurtful to me, I go to him or her and say, "When you said that, this is how I took it—I don't know if that's how you meant it, but that's how I received it and how it made me feel." This kind of low-key confrontation is far less threatening than accusing someone by saying, "This is what you said to me, and this is what you meant by it!"

Many times, our fear is that when we confront people with how their words affected us, their response may be, "You're right! I think you're a total idiot!" But at least if they respond like this, then we've actually got a good reason to cry! It is more likely, however, that they won't say that. Instead, the misunderstanding can usually be ironed out, and a relationship can be saved (maybe even deepened).

It is not a sin to disagree with someone. Nor is it wrong to confront someone. We can have conflict with others, disagree with them, confront them and still remain in unity. Unity does not mean that everyone should say and do exactly the same things. Unity is not necessarily uniformity; it is a heart issue that involves our commitment to love one another, even if we don't see eye to eye on particular issues.

God has a direct answer to the problem of self-talk, as well as many of the other masks that continue to undermine our ability to be all He has created us to be:

> Finally, brethren, whatever is true, whatever is honorable, whatever is right, whatever is pure, whatever is lovely, whatever is of good repute, if there is any excellence and if anything worthy of praise—dwell on these things.
>
> Philippians 4:8

These are the things that ought to fill our minds. Even though we cannot automatically stop thoughts from indiscriminately entering our heads, we can choose what we dwell upon. Successfully dwelling on the truth of God's Word will give us a tremendous advantage in being able to live our lives without masks.

Chapter 10

Working It Out:
Practical Steps to
Changing Your Self-Image

In chapter 6, I related the account of the day that God changed my life. I'll never forget that day on the fourth floor of LIFE Bible College. I remember it so well that I could take you to the exact seat in which I was sitting when Jesus confronted the strongholds in my life. Something broke inside of me that day, and the process of healing and deliverance began.

While I received a miraculous touch at that time, it was only the beginning of my restoration. As the foundational lies in my life were exposed and the strongholds began to break, there were practical steps I needed to take that were essential to my freedom.

Once we understand and have worked through the things that have shaped how we think about ourselves, there are some practical steps we can take in order to change our self-images. It is important to note, however, that we are not referring to changing our identity. That has already been changed in Jesus Christ. Remember, in Christ you have a new identity. You are a new person. Your challenge is to apply that truth to how you see yourself and then begin to live out that truth.

There are certain principles that work well in helping us bring our self-image more in line with God's purpose for our lives.

1. Where It All Begins—A Relationship with Jesus

Man's identity crisis began when Adam sinned and broke his relationship with God, the source of his identity. Jesus came to redeem lost man and restore him to God's intended purpose. Therefore, the only way for man's true identity to be restored is through Christ. Man, without Christ, continues in his fallen state and broken image.

When you receive Christ as Savior, the Scriptures teach that you become a new creation. You have a new identity (see 2 Corinthians 5:17): Your identity is in Christ. While there are great things that psychologists and counselors can do to help you change your self-image (the way you see yourself), only God can change your identity. Only Jesus promises to make a new person out of you and let you start life over again with a clean slate. That's the message of the Gospel. That's why Jesus came.

Without the foundation of a new identity, any attempt to build a new self-image for ourselves will be flawed. Without the foundation stone of Jesus in our lives, we are simply the same old person, trying to make ourselves better and more acceptable. Such attempts are doomed to failure. Without Christ, we cannot have a new identity, and our self-image will continue to be marred by the effects of sin.

The effect of sin in the lives of human beings is volatile and damaging. The only way sin can be truly dealt with and its damaging consequences repaired is through Jesus Christ. He allowed His blood to be shed so that we could be cleansed from the pollution of sin in our lives.

This is why it is important to have not only a personal relationship with Christ, but a growing relationship with

Him. The more we grow in our understanding of who God is and what He is like, the more He lives His life through us, and the more we see ourselves in the light of who He made us to be: His sons and daughters. Therefore, to change our self-image, we must first begin with a personal, growing relationship with Jesus.

2. Getting to Know Your Father

Do you remember the story in chapter 5 about the woman who had been abused by her alcoholic father? She had been a believer for over fifty years and had a deep love for Jesus. When she spoke about God, she often equated His qualities with those of her mother, a gentle and caring woman. On the other hand, to speak of God as a loving, compassionate Father was a great struggle for her.

Because of the experiences in her childhood, this woman equated the cruelty and abuse of her earthly father with the qualities of her heavenly Father, and her relationship with God was limited by her perspective of Him.

It is necessary to realize that there is no such thing as a perfect father—except for God. In order to overcome the perspectives that may limit our relationship with Him, we need to discover what He is really like. Many good books have been written about the character and the fatherhood of God, but there is nothing more powerful than God's Word itself. The Bible tells us what our heavenly Father is like—and ultimately, He is the source of our identity.

There are certain characteristics of God that directly relate to changing the way we think and feel about ourselves. For example:

- God is the King of the universe (see 1 Chronicles 29:11–12; 2 Chronicles 20:6; Psalm 24:8), and therefore, all the circumstances in my life are ultimately in His hand.

- God is righteous (see Psalm 119:137). He cannot sin against me.

- God is just (see Deuteronomy 32:4). He will always be fair to me.

- God is love (see 1 John 4:8). He wants to help me get the most out of my life.

- God is eternal (see Deuteronomy 33:27). The plan He is working out for me is an everlasting plan.

- God is truth (see Psalm 31:5). He cannot lie to me.

- God is everywhere (see Psalm 139:7–10). There is no place I can go that He will not be able to care for me.

- God is all-powerful (see Job 42:2). There is nothing too great for Him to accomplish.

- God is unchangeable (see Malachi 3:6). I can depend on Him.

- God is faithful (see Exodus 34:6; Romans 15:5). I can trust Him to fulfill His promises.

- God is holy (see Revelation 15). He will be holy in all His acts.

God has an infinite number of characteristics and qualities that have a significant impact upon who we are and who He desires us to be. Those I have listed here give only a small picture of what God our Father is like. I encourage you to grow in your understanding of His character. There is great security in walking in close relationship with the loving heavenly Father.

Another way to get to know the Father God is to get to know His Son. Jesus is the visible image of the invisible God. One of His disciples once requested, " 'Lord, show us the Father, and it is enough for us.' Jesus said to him, ' . . . He who has seen Me has seen the Father' " (John 14:8–9). If we are going to grow in our understanding of what God is like, we can do no better than to start by looking at Jesus, the person God sent to reveal Himself to us.

The more we grow in our understanding of who God is and what He is like, the more security it will bring to our hearts, and the more we will understand who He has made us to be. The Creator of the universe is our Father. We have entered into relationship with an awesome God. If this does not tell us something about our value, if it does not foster a sense of security, nothing will. Understanding who God is and what He is like gives us a clear picture of our value and who we are in Him. If we want to change our self-images, the place to start is to grow in our understanding of the character of God.

3. Truth Works Best When Believed

Although we may say we believe the Bible is the infallible Word of God, when our feelings contradict biblical truth, all too often we choose to believe our feelings. In the appendix at the back of this book is a list of 69 statements the Bible makes about who we are. When reading these Scriptures, it is important for us to see ourselves in them, accept what has been written about us and believe what God has said about how He sees us. Only then can we begin to overcome our deceptive and decidedly unreliable feelings.

When we make the choice to allow God's truth to fill our minds, over time our emotions will reflect this choice. Our old negative thoughts will begin to fade away. Our emotions will respond to the truth of God's Word. This does not mean that we should pretend our feelings are non-existent or be surprised when we experience a rush of emotion. But we must recognize that our feelings are not infallible: They can be deceiving. And so we need to evaluate what our feelings tell us, holding them up to the scrutiny of God's Word in order to discern our inward motives.

The truth of God's Word needs to become our constant companion. It needs to become the rod against which we measure all our thoughts and feelings.

4. Fill Your Mind with the Word of God

> This book of the Law shall not depart from your mouth, but you shall meditate on it day and night, so that you may be careful to do according to all that is written in it; for then you will make your way prosperous, and then you will have success.
>
> Joshua 1:8

Several years ago, while I was directing Teen Challenge in Los Angeles, the Lord taught me a lesson in the power of His Word that I will never forget. Shortly after I took over running the program, I met a young man whose mind had all but been destroyed by LSD. A prominent hospital had even tested him and had told his parents there was nothing more anyone could do for him. His brain had been permanently damaged. According to the medical experts, the best thing his parents could do for their son was to institutionalize him, since they would not be able to care for him at home.

This young man wasn't violent, but he was difficult to control. He would do things such as get up in the middle of the night, go for a walk and then forget where he lived. He would see a house that looked similar to his, go up to the door and try to get in. If that didn't work, he would walk around the house looking for the window he thought was his bedroom window and try to climb inside. It was a dangerous thing to do in Los Angeles!

His parents looked around for an institution where their son could be cared for. Eventually they settled on Teen Challenge because of its family environment. They weren't

Christians, and when they came to us, I made it clear we operated a Christian program that employed biblical principles. They said to me, "The doctors tell us that mentally, our son is a vegetable. Your religion certainly isn't going to hurt him any."

We really should not have taken him in. Teen Challenge was a drug rehabilitation program, and there was obviously no rehabilitation for this young man. But I agreed to take him in because I felt God say to me, *Do it.*

Our chaplain at the time got the idea that God was going to restore this young man's mind, and so she decided that student volunteers would read the Bible aloud to him until he was able to memorize the verses. I was skeptical—he couldn't put his first and last names together. How was he ever going to memorize Scripture?

But despite my skepticism, the student volunteers took their new assignment seriously. One of them would read for half an hour and then take a break while someone else would read. That went on each day for weeks.

After several weeks, we began to notice a change. The young man began to follow along in his Bible as the students read to him. It wasn't too long after that he began to memorize passages of Scripture. While his mind was immersed in the Bible, God began restoring other areas of his brain. Finally, fifteen months after arriving at Teen Challenge, he entered one of the leading universities in California.

I haven't heard from him for several years now, but the last time we communicated, he told me he had graduated and taken up a job with the U.S. government, working in a drug rehabilitation program. Love and prayers undoubtedly helped him, but despite my initial skepticism, I am convinced it was the Word of God constantly spoken into his mind that transformed him. If the Word of God can renew a mind so devastated by drugs, imagine what God can do in your mind if you meditate upon His Word.

First of all, the process of meditation begins by *reading the Word of God*. In this technological age with the Bible on tape, Bible-related software or other tools of convenience (all of which can be very helpful), there is still nothing that can really take the place of opening your Bible, getting your nose into it and reading it for yourself. If you think you can place a cassette player with the Bible on tape under your pillow at night and expect that to fulfill your time alone with the Lord, you are sadly mistaken. The Bible is meant to be read, considered, prayed about, spoken and applied in personal fashion. There is no way to get around that.

When I was in Bible college, I loved to read about church history. Biographies of people like John Wesley, John Calvin and Charles Spurgeon were always interesting to me. Their lives inspired me to passionately embrace my relationship with the Lord. Wesley's biography, in particular, was notable in that much of his spiritual strength could be attributed to the fact that he got up every morning at 4:00 A.M. to study the Bible and pray for four hours. His example affected me so much, I decided I would attempt to do the same thing.

Four A.M. seemed a little early for me. I felt I could compromise a bit and set my alarm for 5:00. On the first morning, when my alarm went off, I rolled out of bed and eagerly got on my knees, embarking upon my four-hour prayer marathon. Within minutes, however, I was sound asleep. I awoke a few minutes later, shook my head, wiped my eyes and proceeded to engage in prayer again. I was determined to reach that four-hour goal. Unfortunately, my eyes soon got heavy, and sure enough, I dozed off a second time. Minutes later, I opened my eyes again, got up and splashed some water in my face. I then got back down on my knees and began to pray for everything I could think of. But when I glanced over at my alarm clock, I realized it was only 5:15 A.M. My struggle had gone on for only ten minutes!

I still had three hours and forty-five minutes left to pray and study. My heart sank. Defeated, I crawled back under the covers and went back to sleep.

For two more weeks, I consistently awoke at 5:00 in the morning and tried to conduct my quiet time with the Lord. As determined as I was to follow Wesley's example, however, I could not maintain that schedule. I felt frustrated and condemned by my lack of discipline.

Over the years, I learned that I could conduct my quiet time at hours more appropriate for my body clock. But not too long after that first experience, I was in England and visited the church where John Wesley had preached. I took a tour of the church, which included a stroll through his home, situated right next door. A guide led me into his home and to a large closet with a window in it. This was Wesley's prayer closet. In the floor were grooves that were said to have been made by Wesley's knees as he knelt to pray, morning after morning. I was quite humbled by this.

As I stood quietly for a moment, contemplating what it took for this godly man to accomplish this day in and day out, I turned to my guide and recounted my experience of trying to imitate Wesley's discipline. To my surprise, the guide laughed.

"I can't tell you how many times I've heard that from people," he said. "What they don't tell you in the books, though, is that back in those days, there was no electricity. In England in winter, it gets dark by 5:00 P.M., sometimes even by 4:30. People would light their candles for a while, but usually, they were in bed by 7:00 P.M.!"

I paused, and then it dawned on me. If Wesley went to bed at 7:00 P.M. and slept until 4:00, he had slept for nine hours! Here I was going to bed sometime between midnight or 1:00 and trying to get up about five hours later. No wonder I had been unsuccessful! In fact, Wesley almost seemed lazy to me when I looked at it from this new perspective!

I share this story because it is easy to feel condemned when we know we should be reading the Word and praying, yet all the activities of our day seem to encroach onto that time. It would be wonderful if we could spend an hour or two a day before the Lord every single day, but most of us should begin by setting goals that are more attainable. Being consistent in this discipline is not easy, but most of us can manage praying or meditating upon a few verses for five minutes a day. Then, once we begin to accomplish that on a regular basis, we can try to increase our time to ten minutes, then fifteen and so on.

I also learned from my guide that Wesley did not start out praying for four hours a day; he grew into it. The key is not in the amount of time we spend on devotions, but in the value we place upon it. If we value our time with God, we, too, can grow into a discipline that is significant, more than just time spent.

Second, it is important not only to read the Word, but also to *study* it. Many of us spend too much time examining principles and not enough time examining the Word itself. We need to be students of the Word. Principles will not change your life, but the Word of God will. This is not to say that principles are not worth studying, but it is not enough to study principles alone. Studying the Word of God is an essential part of discipleship.

When you sit down to study the Bible, there are four things to remember. First of all, *determine what the verse you are studying says*. On face value, what does the passage actually say?

Then, *determine what the verse means*. What is the context in which it was written? Is there a historical significance? To what does it refer? Is there any symbolic meaning to what it says?

Third, *determine what the verse means to you on a personal level*. Not only did God speak to His people at the time the verse was written, He also uses His Word to speak to us today. How does the Scripture impact your life in the here and now?

Finally, *determine what you are going to do about it.* The Word of God is not given just to be read or studied—it was given to be obeyed and acted upon. How will the verse change the way you conduct your life?

Memorizing the Word of God can also be of tremendous benefit in restoring your self-concept. At one point in my life I worked as a driver for a diaper service. I had been a youth pastor for some time, and this was something I did in order to make ends meet between pastorships. I was known, during that time, as "Dirty Dan, the Diaper Man."

Nevertheless, I found there was one aspect of this job that was a tremendous spiritual blessing. I would get small three-by-five index cards and write Scripture verses on them. Then I would tape the card on the visor of my truck at the beginning of the day and work on memorizing the verses as I drove my route. All day long, I would continue to go back to that Scripture. I would read it, meditate upon it, speak it, even sing the verse. In other words, I would do anything I could to help myself to memorize the verse until it became part of me.

The following morning, I would quickly go through the previous day's Scripture and then write down a new one so I could go through the process all over again. During those months, I memorized dozens and dozens of verses. To this day, I feel I have retained probably about 80 to 85 percent of the verses I memorized back then. If the Word of God is in your mind, you will have it with you wherever you go. Therefore, it is important to memorize Scripture.

Fourth, *picture the Word of God.* This is a fun thing to do, especially if you have a good imagination. Indeed, imagination is truly a gift from God. When used in a way that glorifies Him, it can be a tremendous blessing. There are some who quote the verse that talks about "casting down imaginations" (see 2 Corinthians 10:5), as if to indicate that using one's imagination is somehow evil. Put in context, however, this verse refers to an imagination that exalts itself above God. If you are using your imagination for sinful things, then, by all means, it must be cast down. But God gave us the ability to function creatively, and we should not try to stop using our imagination. We need to redeem it and use it for good purposes.

What I would do in order to picture the Word, for instance in Joshua 1:8, is imagine the Lord speaking that word to Joshua among the Israelites out in the desert. I try to imagine how it must have looked at the time. Then I take it one step further: I picture myself hearing the Word and acting upon it. I believe that is where faith begins. I see myself becoming a man who speaks the Word, meditates upon the Word and puts it into action. I picture myself doing what God tells me to do.

A friend of mine was once flying an airplane and flew into a storm. He recounted to me that the flight got pretty rough, and before he knew it, pictures flashed across his mind of his plane crashing and his wife and children standing at the end of the runway waiting for him, only to hear that his plane had crashed. He had visions of how devastated they would be. He told me that fear gripped him because it was, indeed, the type of storm in which something like that could happen.

He soon found himself making decisions as he was flying the plane that he knew were wrong, but because he had become so afraid, he was not thinking clearly. In a sense, he was ensuring that what he was afraid of would come upon him. He suddenly caught himself and declared, "I am not going to do this!"

He began to work with his imagination so that, instead of picturing the worst, he pictured himself going through the storm, landing the plane safely and meeting his family at the end of the runway, throwing his arms around them in joyful embrace. And that is exactly what happened. When he changed the picture in his mind, he was at peace, which gave him the stability to think clearly and make the correct decisions. Had he not changed his thought processes, his decisions would have been based on fear, which can lead to cloudy judgment and negative results.

Finally, it is important to *allow the Word of God to reshape your thinking.* You have the ability to change your mind, to change the way you think.

I am convinced that one of the major keys to being obedient to the Lord is having our minds full of the Word of God. The battle that rages within us is between what our natural minds say about us and what God says about us. However, the more we fill our minds with the Word of God, the more we begin to think like God and see things from His perspective.

5. Forgive Those Who Have Hurt You

In chapter 7, we discussed the issue of forgiveness, one of the most fundamental and important issues for us if we are to walk in the power of the new identity God has given us. Unless we forgive, we will never be free. It is that simple. God's forgiveness of us and our forgiveness of others is what the Gospel message is all about.

Whether wounds are inflicted intentionally or unintentionally upon me, it is still my responsibility to forgive. I base this not on my feelings or emotional response. I forgive because God has commanded me to do so. If my desire is to find true freedom and be able to move beyond the past, unforgiveness is not an option.

6. Forget about It!

"Do not remember the former things,
Nor consider the things of old.
Behold, I will do a new thing,
Now it shall spring forth;
Shall you not know it?"

Isaiah 43:18–19, NKJV

In other words, Isaiah was saying, don't spend your time dwelling on the past, but rather look at what God wants to do with you in the future. You should not keep rehashing in your mind the negative things that have happened to you. There comes a point, after dealing with a past situation, when you must forget it and go on with your life.

Forgetting, however, does not mean ignoring continual problems or pretending as if something never happened. That is simply not an emotionally healthy thing to do. When I refer to forgetting, I mean that you have faced the problem, forgiven where forgiveness was needed and asked forgiveness when you have offended. You have dealt with that situation. It is over and done.

> Brothers, I do not consider myself yet to have taken hold of it. But one thing I do: Forgetting what is behind and straining toward what is ahead, I press on toward the goal to win the prize for which God has called me heavenward in Christ Jesus.
>
> Philippians 3:13–14, NIV

Like most of us, Paul faced painful situations in his life, many of them in relationship to his ministry, some of them even at the hands of his own converts. On top of that, I'm sure the memory of Stephen being stoned to death while Paul held the cloaks of those doing the stoning would be haunting. As a result of his own zealousness for Judaism, a number of men and women were put to death. But Paul dealt with his past. He sought forgiveness, and he walked in the power of the new identity God gave to him. As a result, he was able to hold his head up and write that he was forgetting what was behind and reaching toward the goal to win the prize for which God had called him heavenward in Christ Jesus.

Tragically, many of us choose to live in past hurt, disappointments and failure. The mistakes of yesterday are still governing our lives today and destroying our tomorrows. It's time to let them go!

We must learn to deal with the issues of our past and then get on with our lives. Stop wallowing in the same old garbage. Receive healing and move on.

7. Seeing Yourself as God Sees You

In chapter 8, we discussed the story of Gideon. The angel of the Lord appeared to Gideon as he was beating out wheat in the winepress and declared him to be a mighty man of valor. Gideon, however, saw himself as a coward, hiding in the winepress so the Midianite raiders couldn't find him.

The angel of the Lord affirmed and declared Gideon to be something that, in the natural, he was not. God does the same with us. He declares us to be who He has created us to be. Then, as the angel of the Lord did with Gideon, He will walk us to the point where we can fulfill what He has declared us to be.

How does God see our past?

> If we confess our sins, He is faithful and righteous to forgive us our sins and to cleanse us from all unrighteousness.
>
> 1 John 1:9

> As far as the east is from the west,
> So far has He removed our transgressions from us.
>
> Psalm 103:12

God sees us now as His children.

> See how great a love the Father has bestowed on us, that we would be called children of God; and such we are.
>
> 1 John 3:1–2

> God made Him who knew no sin to be sin on our behalf, so that we might become the righteousness of God in Him.
>
> 2 Corinthians 5:21

God sees our future.

> Eye has not seen, nor ear heard,
> Nor have entered into the heart of man
> The things which God has prepared for those who love Him.
>
> 1 Corinthians 2:9, NKJV

> "He who overcomes, I will grant to him to sit down with Me on My throne, as I also overcame and sat down with My Father on His throne."
>
> Revelation 3:21

> "[The Lamb has] made us kings and priests to our God;
> And we shall reign on the earth."
>
> Revelation 5:10, NKJV

8. Accept and Appreciate Who God Has Made You to Be

There is no one else like you, and God has a unique plan and purpose that only you can fulfill.

God has endowed each of us with a unique combination of gifts and limitations that ensure us a special position within the Body of Christ. In His infinite creativity, God has fashioned the Body in such a way that I need you and you need me. I have talents and abilities that you do not have. Likewise, you have talents and abilities I do not possess. My limitations are someone else's strengths, and vice versa.

Therefore, it is important to work diligently to develop the gifts and abilities God has given you. When you employ your gifts and talents, you glorify and honor Him.

> Do not neglect the gift that is in you, which was given to you by prophecy with the laying on of the hands of the eldership. Meditate on these things; give yourself entirely to them, that your progress may be evident to all. Take heed to yourself and to the doctrine. Continue in them, for in doing this you will save both yourself and those who hear you.
>
> 1 Timothy 4:14–16

Paul instructed Timothy not to ignore the talents and abilities that God had given him. He encouraged him to embrace those gifts and nurture them so that they would be fully developed.

It is in your talents and abilities in which you will excel. But you cannot become an expert overnight—even spiritual gifts need to be cultivated. Even though all of your gifts may be natural, if you fail to work at developing them, you will never be able to use them to the full degree that God intends you to use them.

People often ask me, "How do I know what my gifts are?" My answer is very practical. What do you enjoy doing? What is it that you want to accomplish in your life? I am not referring to career aspirations or recreational activities. What are the things you do in your life that bring you the most satisfaction and fulfillment? Do you enjoy making new friends? Are you excited when you organize a party? Do you feel good when you meet someone else's need? Your answers will be related to your personal gifting.

Many people believe that if you really desire and enjoy something, God must be against it. But God is not a hard taskmaster. When it comes to the area of gifting and life direction, if your heart is truly seeking after the Lord, you will find that your heartfelt desires are God-given.

What do other people say about you? What gifts do they recognize in you? Ask them. Find out what they think. Friends can offer a unique perspective. They see you in ways you are unable to see yourself. Take what they tell you and bring it before the Lord. Pray and ask Him to confirm to your heart whether or not their insights are right.

Likewise, you may wish to take one of the many tests designed to help people discover their strengths and weaknesses. Tests like these have been developed to give us some indication as to what our gifts, talents and abilities may be. Although their results may not be absolutely conclusive, they can be a good indicator of where your interests lie.

Above all, step out and see what happens. If you feel a certain pull toward one or more gifts, talents or abilities, get involved in activities or ministries that utilize them. Often you won't know what you can do until you've tried. You may even have to experiment a little in order to see the situation clearly.

Once you have taken such a step, evaluate your experience. Was what you did fruitful? Did you experience a sense of fulfillment as you used a particular gift or talent? If you look objectively at the situation, you may be able to discover a whole new avenue of fulfillment that you may have never before considered.

The talents and abilities that we have are God's gifts to us—but what we do with them is our gift to God. Therefore, it is important not just to determine the gifts He has given you, but also to develop those gifts. In 1 Timothy 4:14–16, Paul gave five instructions about your gifts:

1. **Do not neglect them.**

2. **Be diligent to develop them.**

3. **Give yourself wholly to them.**

4. **Pay close attention to your life and doctrine.**

5. **Persevere in them**.

Learning to accept and appreciate the gifts that God has given you also means learning to accept and appreciate your limitations. You cannot do everything well, and that's okay. God has constructed the Body of Christ in such a way that I need you and you need me. I have talents and abilities you do not have, and you have talents and abilities that I don't have. We need each other.

Our limitations can, in fact, build strength into our lives. They force us to daily rely upon Jesus, and they require that we gather people around us who can make up for our areas of weakness. Without limitations, we wouldn't need each other. But the more we understand our limitations, the more we can appreciate others and what God can bring into our lives through them.

9. Be Determined, Yet Patient with Yourself

I am determined to become all God wants me to become. But I know this will not happen overnight. It takes time. God is doing a progressive work within me. I will eventually become all that God has created me to be, but I also need to be patient with myself in the meantime.

I have seen too many Christians say to themselves, *I'm going to be everything God wants me to be*, but after a week goes by and nothing changes in their lives, they say, "It didn't work for me, so forget it!"

It takes time and determination to see God fulfill His purposes within you. Measure the changes that take place in your life in years, not days or weeks. It is a long-term, ongoing process that may last the rest of your life.

Not long before his death, Winston Churchill was asked to identify the secret of his success. He glared at his audience with his bulldog face and growled, "Never give up!"

Thomas Edison experimented over a thousand times before he successfully developed the light bulb. One night, he was summoned to his laboratory because the structure had caught fire and was burning to the ground. All of his experiments, papers and equipment had gone up in flames. As he stood there watching, the onlookers asked him, "What will you do now?"

"We're going to start rebuilding in the morning!" came his immediate response.

Edison was a man who was determined, yet he was also patient. Determine to keep moving forward in God. Be patient with yourself. Continually remind yourself not to give up. God will never give up on you, so why give up on yourself? God has a lifetime of work to perform in our lives. Each day that passes, you become more and more like Jesus. You are not the same person you were when you first believed.

10. Learn to Serve

I have found over the years that it is important to remind myself who the gifts God has given me are actually for. The gifts really are not for me. They are for the person to whom I am ministering—given in order to bless or help him or her. I am merely the conduit, the messenger God uses to touch the life of another person.

Knowing this kicks the rug out from under my pride. I have never noticed my mailman getting puffed up with pride over delivering the mail to my house. He is merely the medium by which my mail gets to me. If you see your gifts, talents and abilities as means for your own personal gain, they will only lead to pride. But if you seek to use your particular gifts for the gain of others, they will lead to fulfillment.

In fact, one of the reasons it is so important to understand your new identity is for the purpose of serving others. I once heard the word *servant* defined as "one who spends his or her life making others successful."

Like most young pastors, I struggled for success, and I believe I have achieved a reasonable degree of it. But over the years, I've discovered something far more important. The more I invest in the success of others, the more successful I become. Isn't that what ministry is all about in the first place? Jesus said that if you seek to save your life, you'll lose it. But if you give your life away, you will find it (see Matthew 16:25). This is a fundamental principle of God's Kingdom. Investing our lives in the success of other people is ultimately where we will find true success. It is that simple. God's desire is to bless the world through His Church.

Many people spend their entire lives struggling with the question, "Who am I?" They become preoccupied with trying to figure out the answer. But the more you understand who you truly are, the less preoccupied you will be with yourself, and the more you can get on with the job God has called and equipped you to do. The more you understand who you are in Jesus, the more you will be set free to reach out and touch a desperately needy world—a world that longs to hear God's message of love, acceptance and forgiveness.

Chapter 11

Free at Last!

O God most high, almighty King
The Champion of Heaven, Lord of everything
You've fought, You've won, death's lost its sting
And standing in Your victory we sing
You have broken the chains
That held our captive souls
You have broken the chains
And used them on your foes
All Your enemies are bound
They tremble at the sound of Your Name
Jesus, You have broken the chains
The power of hell has been undone
Captivity held captive by the Risen One
And in the name of God's great Son
We claim the mighty victory You've won
You have broken the chains
That held our captive souls
You have broken the chains
And used them on Your foes
All Your enemies are bound
They tremble at the sound of Your Name
Jesus, You have broken the chains
Jesus, You have broken the chains
Jesus, You have broken the chains![1]

[1] Jamie Owens Collins, "You Have Broken the Chains." Copyright © 1990 by Fairhill Music, Inc. ASCAP. Used by permission. All rights reserved. International copyright secured.

The chains that have held you fast and kept you from fulfilling all that God desires for your life have been broken. You have a new identity that has been secured for you by the blood of Jesus Christ. All the pain of your past, the strongholds of your life and the foundational lies that have plagued you are shattered. You are free at last!

When Secretary Seward placed the Emancipation Proclamation on the desk of Abraham Lincoln for his signature, the president took a pen, dipped it in ink and moved his hand to the space for his signature. But then he paused momentarily and removed his hand, dropping the pen without signing. Hesitating for a moment longer, he picked the pen back up and prepared to sign the document once again.

President Lincoln turned to Mr. Seward and explained, "I have been shaking hands since nine o'clock this morning, and my arm is almost paralyzed. If my name ever goes into history, it will be for this act, and my whole soul is in it. If my hand trembles when I sign the proclamation, all who examine the document hereafter will say, 'He hesitated.' "

The president turned back to the document and firmly and deliberately signed his name, "Abraham Lincoln," in the sloping scrawl with which the world is now familiar. Lincoln then looked up from the document, smiled and said, "That will do." A pen dipped in ink and the signature of Abraham Lincoln had ended legalized slavery in the United States forever.

But history tells us that even after the proclamation was signed, thousands continued to live as slaves, perhaps out of ignorance, confusion or fear. They remained in bondage even though they had legally been set free. What a tragedy! Slavery was all they had known. The meaning of freedom was a difficult concept to grasp for those who had never known what freedom was like. The question arose, "How do we live as free people?"

To a great degree, this was also true of the first generation of the children of Israel as they sought the Promised Land. They had lived in slavery all of their lives, and when the chains were broken, they were free from oppression—free from the bonds that had kept them from fulfilling God's desire for them as His people. Yet now that they were free, how would they live?

> "Every place on which the sole of your foot treads shall be yours; your border will be from the wilderness to Lebanon, and from the river, the river Euphrates, as far as the western sea."
>
> Deuteronomy 11:24

The first time I read that verse, it seemed to me that it contained a significant contradiction. On the one hand, the Israelites were promised that every place that the soles of their feet stepped would be given to them by God. But on the other hand, they were clearly told that He had set boundaries for them: "from the wilderness to Lebanon, and from the river . . . Euphrates, as far as the western [or Mediterranean] sea."

What first appears to be a contradiction, however, proves not to be so. In reality, these two ideas were two sides of the same coin, or different perspectives of the same promise. It could be said that one side represented God's responsibility and the other represented the responsibility of Israel. God intended Israel to possess a geographical piece of land within the set boundaries He had established. From that location, the Israelites could fulfill their intended purpose to become a people of worship and to bless all the nations of the world. This was His promise to them.

But while God promised that He would give them this land, He also required that they go in and possess it, step by step. It was theirs, but they had to put their footprints on it! God promised that He would go before them and drive out the current inhabitants, but the children of Israel still had to put their mark upon the land. In reality, they had to discover and develop the gifts God had given to them. They were God's chosen people. That was who they were. Now God required them to inhabit the fullness of His promise and become everything He desired them to be.

It is sobering to note that, to this day, the nation of Israel has never fully inhabited the boundaries of the land God promised them. The closest Israel ever came to doing so was in the days of King David. Theirs is a tremendous example of how difficult it is to overcome the mentality of slavery. In fact, the first generation of the children of Israel never inhabited the Promised Land at all—with two notable exceptions, Joshua and Caleb.

In chapter 1, we saw how the children of Israel suffered from the "grasshopper syndrome." Joshua and Caleb were among the twelve spies sent to assess the Promised Land and determine what lay ahead of the Israelites as they prepared to inhabit God's promise. These two men saw exactly the same things as the other ten spies. They experienced the same emotions, and they probably felt as intimidated as the others. They saw the giants in the land and knew that they were small in comparison to such odds. But while the other spies considered it impossible for them to overcome the giants, Joshua and Caleb knew that God was with them. They believed God and believed that He had chosen Israel. They knew that God had broken the chains of slavery and that Israel could fulfill all God desired for them. And while the other ten spies and the rest of the first generation of the children of Israel passed away before entering the Promised Land, Joshua and Caleb triumphantly led the next generation into it.

Even though you may now be living in tremendous physical, emotional and spiritual slavery, whether from sin or the painful experiences of the past, you have a bright future ahead of you! There is no chain that God cannot break, no stronghold that God cannot penetrate, no lie that God's truth cannot overcome. In fact, it has already been done!

Allow the Holy Spirit to set you free, and then embrace that freedom with the knowledge that God has freed you to become the person He intended you to be. As God has broken you free from the chains of your past, shake those chains loose. Allow the soles of your feet to tread upon the land of God's promise for your life. As you do, you will not only experience the joy of new life, you will also discover the fulfillment of your potential. The shackles of defeat and weakness will no longer dominate you, and you will enjoy the power of a new identity.

Appendix

Who Am I in Christ?

In Christ, I am:

1. God's child, born again of the incorruptible Seed of the Word of God, that lives and abides forever (1 Peter 1:23)

2. Forgiven of all my sins and washed in the blood (Ephesians 1:7; Colossians 1:14; Hebrews 9:14; 1 John 1:9, 2:12)

3. A new creature (2 Corinthians 5:17)

4. The temple of the Holy Spirit (1 Corinthians 6:19)

5. Delivered from the power of darkness and translated into God's Kingdom (Colossians 1:13)

6. Redeemed from the curse of the law (Galatians 3:13; 1 Peter 1:18–19;)

7. Blessed (Deuteronomy 28:1–4; Galatians 3:9)

8. A saint (Romans 1:7; 1 Corinthians 1:2; Philippians 1:1)

9. The head and not the tail (Deuteronomy 28:13)

10. Above only and not beneath (Deuteronomy 28:13)

11. Holy and without blame before God in love elect (Ephesians 1:4; 1 Peter 1:16)

12. Elect (Romans 8:33; Colossians 3:12)

13. Established to the end (1 Corinthians 1:8)

14. Brought near to God by the blood of Christ (Ephesians 2:13)

15. Victorious (Revelation 2:17)

16. Set free (John 8:31–33)

17. Strong in the Lord (Ephesians 6:10)

18. Dead to sin (Romans 6:2, 11; 1 Peter 2:24)

19. More than a conqueror (Romans 8:37)

20. A joint heir with Christ (Romans 9:17)

21. Sealed with the Holy Spirit of promise (Ephesians 1:13)

22. In Christ Jesus by His doing (1 Corinthians 1:30)

23. Accepted in the beloved (Ephesians 1:6)

24. Complete in Him (Colossians 2:10)

25. Crucified with Christ (Galatians 2:20)

26. Alive with Christ (Ephesians 2:5)

27. Free from condemnation (Romans 8:1)

28. Reconciled to God (1 Corinthians 5:18)

29. Qualified to share in His inheritance (Colossians 1:12)

30. Firmly rooted, built up and established in my faith and overflowing with gratitude (Colossians 2:7)

31. Circumcised with the circumcision made without hands (Colossians 2:11)

32. A fellow citizen with the saints and of the household of God (Ephesians 2:19)

33. Built upon the foundation of the apostles and prophets, Jesus Christ Himself being the Chief Cornerstone (Ephesians 2:20)

34. In the world as He is in heaven (1 John 4:17)

35. Born of God and untouched by the evil one (1 John 5:18)

36. His faithful follower (Ephesians 5:1; Revelation 17:14)

37. Overtaken with blessings (Deuteronomy 28:2; Ephesians 1:3)

38. His disciple because I have love for others (John 13:34–35)

39. The light of the world (Matthew 5:14)

40. The salt of the earth (Matthew 5:13)

41. The righteousness of God (1 Corinthians 5:21; 1 Peter 2:24)

42. A partaker of His divine nature (2 Peter 1:4)

43. Called of God (2 Timothy 1:9)

44. The firstfruits among His creation (James 1:18)

45. Chosen (Ephesians 1:4; 1 Thessalonians 1:4; 1 Peter 2:9)

46. An ambassador for Christ (2 Corinthians 5:20)

47. God's workmanship, created in Christ Jesus for good works (Ephesians 2:10)

48. The apple of my Father's eye (Deuteronomy 32:10; Psalm 17:8)

49. Healed by the stripes of Jesus (Isaiah 53:6; 1 Peter 2:24)

50. Being changed into His image (2 Corinthians 3:18; Philippians 1:6)

51. Raised up with Christ and seated in heavenly places (Ephesians 2:6; Colossians 2:12)

52. Beloved of God (Romans 1:7; Colossians 3:12; 1 Thessalonians 1:4)

53. One in Christ (John 17:21–23)

In Christ, I have:

54. The mind of Christ (1 Corinthians 2:16; Philippians 2:5)

55. Obtained an inheritance (Ephesians 1:11)

56. Access by one Spirit to the Father (Ephesians 2:18; Hebrews 4:16)

57. Overcome the world (1 John 5:4)

58. Everlasting life (John 5:24, 6:47)

59. The peace of God which passes understanding (Philippians 4:7)

60. Received power, the power of the Holy Spirit: power to lay hands on the sick and see them recover, power to cast out demons, power over all the power of the enemy (Mark 16:17–18; Luke 19:17, 19)

In Christ, I live:

61. By the law of the Spirit of life in Christ Jesus (Romans 8:2)

In Christ, I walk:

62. In Christ Jesus (Colossians 2:6)

In Christ, I can:

63. Do all things (Philippians 4:13)

In Christ, I will:

64. Do even greater works than Christ Jesus (Philippians 4:13)

In Christ, I possess:

65. The greater One in me, because greater is He who is in me than he that is in the world (1 John 4:4)

In Christ, I will:

66. Press toward the mark for the prize of the high calling of God (Philippians 3:14)

67. Always triumph in Christ (2 Corinthians 2:14)

68. Show forth His praise (1 Peter 2:9)

In Christ, my life:

69. Is hidden with Christ in God (Colossians 3:3)

About the Author

Dan Sneed has traveled extensively in the United States and abroad as a Bible teacher and conference speaker. Upon graduating from LIFE Bible College, he began his ministry in a small mission church in Los Angeles. Over the years, Dan and his wife, Beverly, have served as pastors and youth pastors in a charismatic Lutheran church. Dan has also served as the director of Los Angeles Teen Challenge and the director of Jesus West Coast—a large, annual evangelism and missions festival in Southern California. Dan and Beverly have also pastored Foursquare churches in Altadena, Northridge and Thousand Oaks, California.

Dan serves as a member of the non-resident faculty at the University of the Nations in Kona, Hawaii, and teaches regularly at Youth With A Mission in their Discipleship Training Schools, Schools of Evangelism, Counseling Schools and various other seminars.

From 1995 through 1999, Dan was the European coordinator for Foursquare Missions International, a branch of the International Church of the Foursquare Gospel, coordinating personnel and ministry in seventeen European nations.

Currently Dan resides in Thousand Oaks, California, with his wife and family, and he travels extensively both nationally and abroad.

About the publisher

We hope you enjoyed reading this Sovereign World book.
For more details of other Sovereign books and
new releases see our website:

www.sovereignworld.com
Find us on Twitter @sovereignworld

Our authors welcome your feedback on their books.
Please send your comments to our offices.
You can request to subscribe to our email and
mailing list online or by writing to:

Sovereign World Ltd
PO Box 784, Ellel, Lancaster, LA1 9DA
United Kingdom

info@sovereignworld.com

Sovereign World titles are available from all good
Christian bookshops and eBook vendors.
For information about our distributors in the UK, USA,
Canada, South Africa, Australia and Singapore, visit:

www.sovereignworld.com/trade

If you would like to help us send a copy of this book and
many other titles to needy pastors in developing countries,
please write for further information or send your gift to:

Sovereign World Trust
PO Box 777, Tonbridge, Kent, TN11 0ZS
United Kingdom

www.sovereignworldtrust.org.uk

The Sovereign World Trust is a registered charity

Lightning Source UK Ltd.
Milton Keynes UK
UKOW06f0200020416

271356UK00001B/29/P